T0037774

C

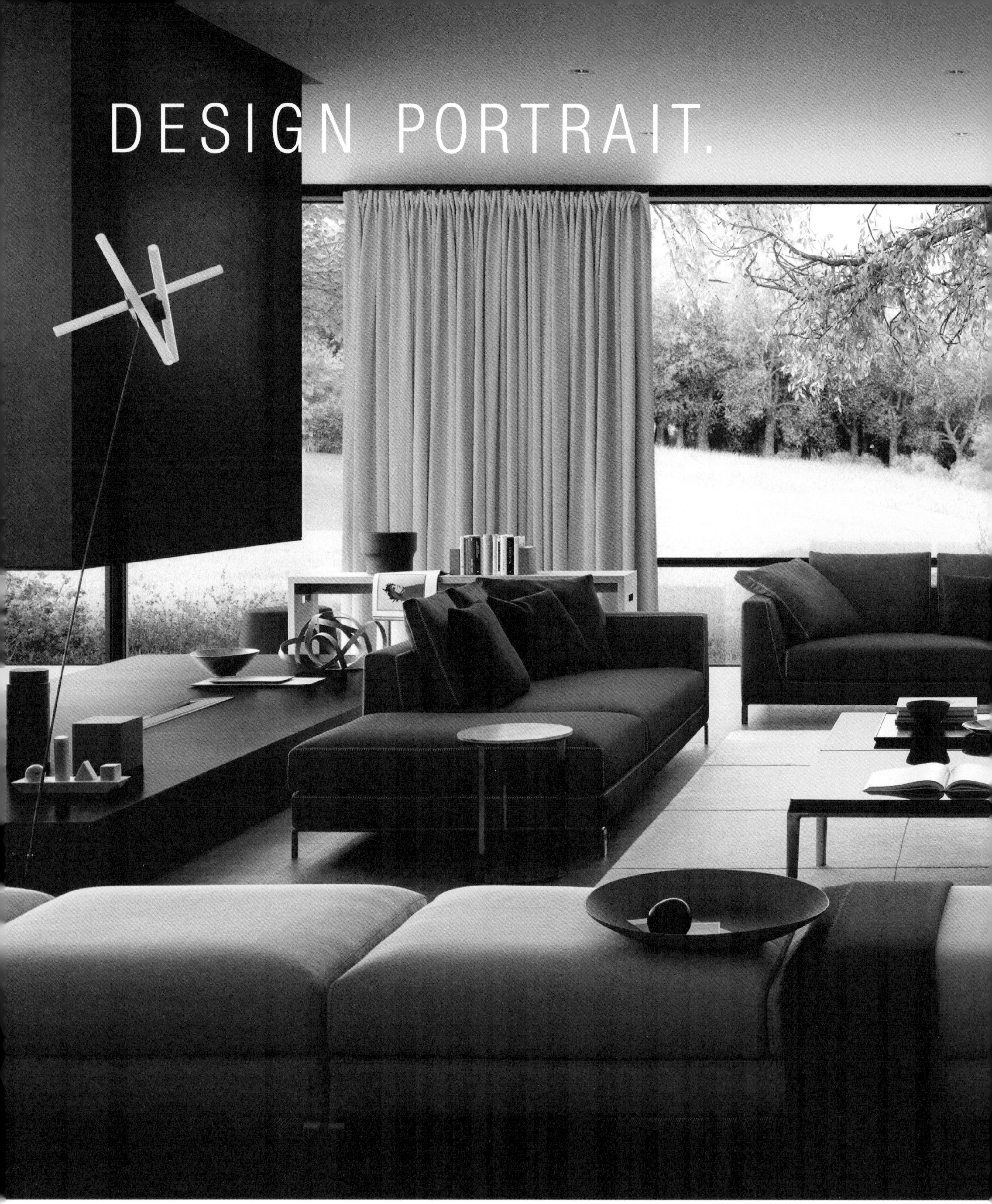

MARAZZI

LAMINAM

At home with perfection.
Created with minimalistic form for maximum impact.

www.bulthaup.com

bulthaup

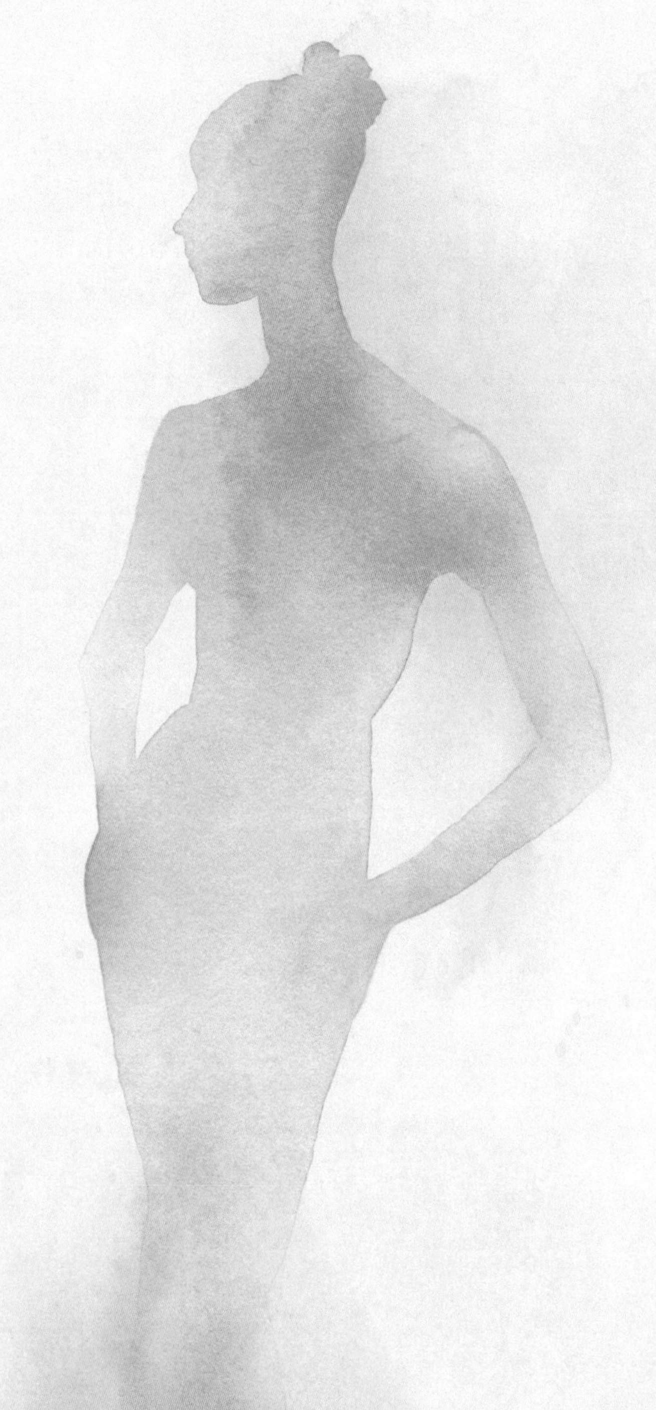

MADEMOISELLE

PROPORTION · LONDON

Contents

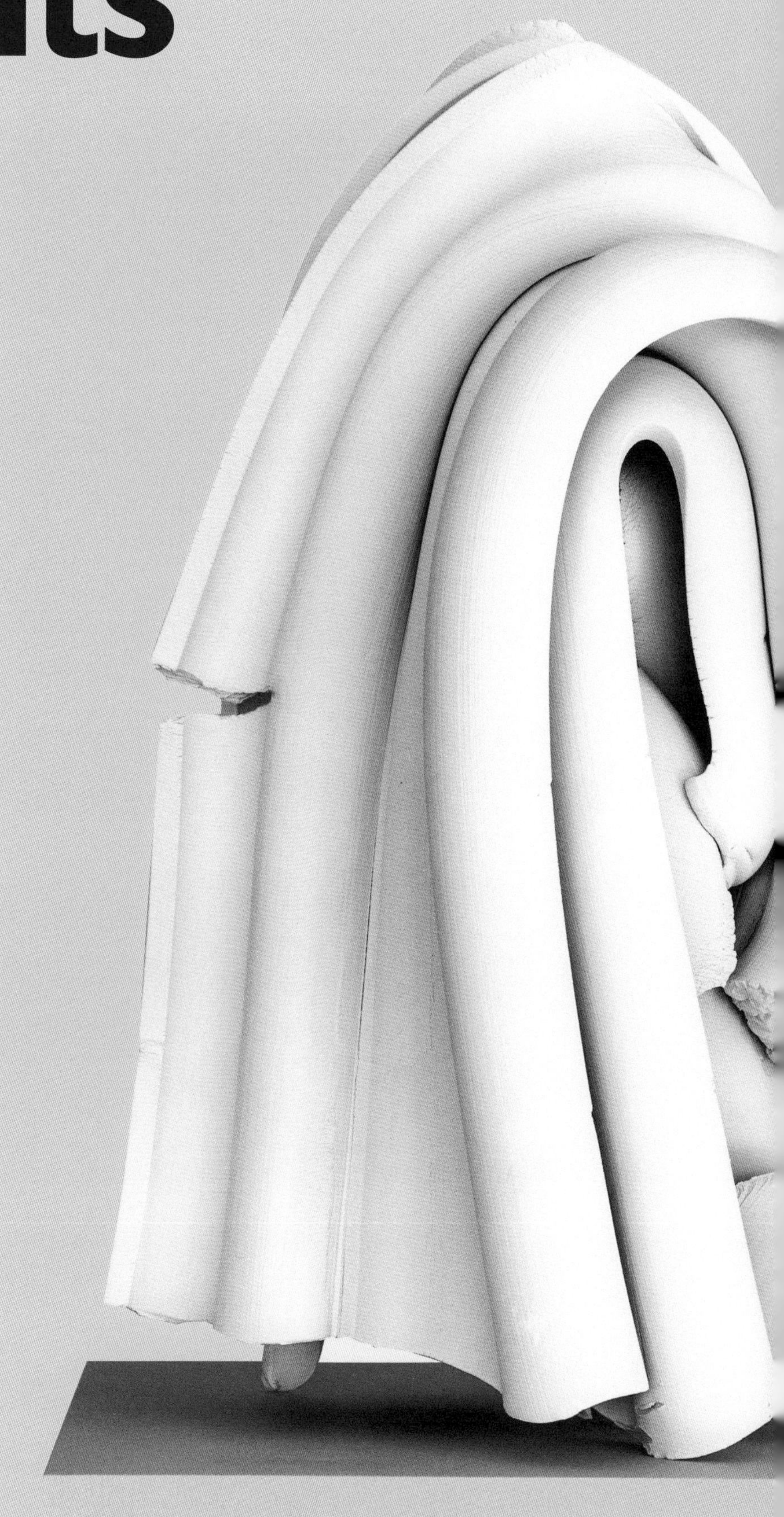

Anton Alvarez and others experiment with making processes on page 32.

Photo Charles Hosea

Universal Design Studio tones it down for J&M Davidson on page 114.

content in the digital magazine

It began with a spark...

***Frame* is published six times a year by**

Frame Publishers
Laan der Hesperiden 68
NL-1076 DX Amsterdam
T +31 20 423 3717
F +31 20 428 0653
frame@frameweb.com
frameweb.com

Editorial

Editor in chief
Robert Thiemann – RT

Managing editor
Tracey Ingram – TI

Editors
Floor Kuitert – FK
Maria Elena Oberti – MEO

Editorial intern
Christian Walters – CW

Copy editors
InOtherWords (D'Laine Camp, Donna de Vries-Hermansader)

Design director
Barbara Iwanicka

Graphic designers
Vincent Hammingh
Cathelijn Kruunenberg

Creative consultant
Alvin Chan

Translation
InOtherWords (Maria van Tol, Rachel Keeton, Donna de Vries-Hermansader)

Contributors to this issue
Alice Blackwood – AB
Nicola Bozzi – NB
Will Georgi – WG
Daniel Golling – DG
Lauren Grieco – LG
Kanae Hasegawa – KH
Ronald Hooft – RH
Melanie Mendelewitsch – MM
Lara Mikocki – LM
Enya Moore – EM
Shonquis Moreno – SM
Jeannette Petrik – JP
Jill Diane Pope – JDP
Bradley Quinn – BQ
Anna Sansom – AS
Jane Szita – JS
Michael Webb – MW
Anne van der Zwaag – AvdZ

Web editor
Lauren Grieco
lauren@frameweb.com

Cover
Image Vincent van Gurp

Lithography
Edward de Nijs

Printing
Grafisch Bedrijf Tuijtel

Publishing

Directors
Robert Thiemann
Rudolf van Wezel

Sales and marketing director
Margreet Nanning
margreet@frameweb.com

Brand manager
Hanneke Stuij
hanneke@frameweb.com

Distribution and logistics
Nick van Oppenraaij
nick@frameweb.com

Finance
Cedric Isselt
cedric@frameweb.com

Pearl Yssel
pearl@frameweb.com

Advertising

Sales managers
Nikki Brandenburg
nikki@frameweb.com

Sarah Maisey
sarahmaisey@frameweb.com

Advertising representatives
Italy
Studio Mitos
Michele Tosato
T +39 0422 894 868
michele@studiomitos.it

Turkey
Titajans
Hilmi Zafer Erdem
T +90 212 257 76 66
titajans@titajans.com

Licence holders
Korea
Tong Yang Media Co. Ltd.
Young Lee
T +82 70 8169 6013
framekorea@gmail.com

Queries
service@frameweb.com

Bookstore distributors
Frame is available at sales points worldwide. Please see frameweb.com/magazines/where-to-buy.

Frame (USPS No: 019-372) is published bimonthly by Frame Publishers NL and distributed in the USA by Asendia USA, 17B South Middlesex Ave., Monroe, NJ 08831. Periodicals postage paid at New Brunswick, NJ, and additional mailing offices.

Postmaster: send address changes to *Frame*, 701C Ashland Ave., Folcroft, PA 19032.

ISSN FRAME: 1388-4239

Subscribe

Regular subscription
From €99
Introductory 1-year subscription
From €79
Student subscription
From €69

Visit frameweb.com/subscribe for more options or e-mail us at service@frameweb.com.

Back issues
Buy online at store.frameweb.com

Employing little more than 'a light and some wires', cover artist Vincent van Gurp puts brands centre stage for this issue's retail theme.

OBJECTS sunglasses from Komono (courtesy of KaDenz), shoe from Jimmy Choo, and perfume from Chanel

> **Include as many brands as you want; all it takes is a single spotlight to present "brands on show"**
>
> Vincent van Gurp

X-Code
Design: Daniel Figueroa
www.dauphin.de
Dauphin HumanDesign® Group
DAUPHIN

What's **New**?

Last summer I acted as external examiner at Switzerland's unrivalled university of art and design, ÉCAL. An honour as well as an inspirational responsibility. Not only did I get to peek behind the scenes at a world-famous academy; I also had a chance to immerse myself in the new ideas of talented youngsters for a few days. One or two projects really caught my eye. I was struck, for example, by a **typeface** with a particularly lucid, open look and – how should I put it? – a fresh, edgy pulse of positivity. We decided to ask the young designer, Tancrède Ottiger, to expand his little family of fonts with the addition of a sans-serif variant. The result appears for the first time in this issue of *Frame*.

We need beginners like Ottiger to lend form to our times and to enrich our culture. The search for emerging and established talent is part of *Frame*'s DNA. Our new collaboration with **Eyes on Talents** is the next logical step. This online Paris-based outfit offers creatives a digital platform, just as we do, but ours is in print. Together we're giving the world's most innovative designers – the award winners – a launch pad for their careers. We're showing their work at international design events, in newsletters, in a dedicated section of the Eyes on Talents site, and in a special end-of-the-year edition of *Frame*. The magazine's new **Talents** section – debuting in this issue – is a sneak preview of what's to come.

An important part of our mission is to create an interactive communication network among established and not-yet-established design talents, makers and users – a source of inspiration for the realization of excellence in spatial design. An event such as Milan Design Week is a consummate venue for introducing such a concept. That's why *Frame* is staging its premier themed exhibition – **What's the Matter? : Design for a phygital world** – at the most important design fair on earth. The show displays the work of some 20 designers and companies that demonstrate how physical and digital are becoming increasingly intertwined – from digital animations featuring morphing materials to solid physical objects that enable digital interaction. Design is no longer one or the other, but more and more often a combination of the virtual and the real. Technology previously embedded in computers is emerging to enter our physical surroundings. Everything around us is getting smarter, from clothes to living rooms and workplaces.

What we need the talents of the future to do, above all else, is to give technology form and meaning.

Robert Thiemann
Editor in chief

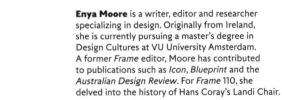

“ The retail industry has an exciting future ahead of it

Bradley Quinn

London's **Bradley Quinn** is a fashion-industry consultant, strategist and lecturer. Specializing in wearable technologies and advanced materials, he is the author of titles such as *TechnoFashion*, *Fashion Futures*, *The Fashion of Architecture*, *UltraMaterials*, *Textile Futures*, *Design Futures* and *Textile Visionaries*. Quinn explores the ins and outs of retail for this issue's Frame Lab.

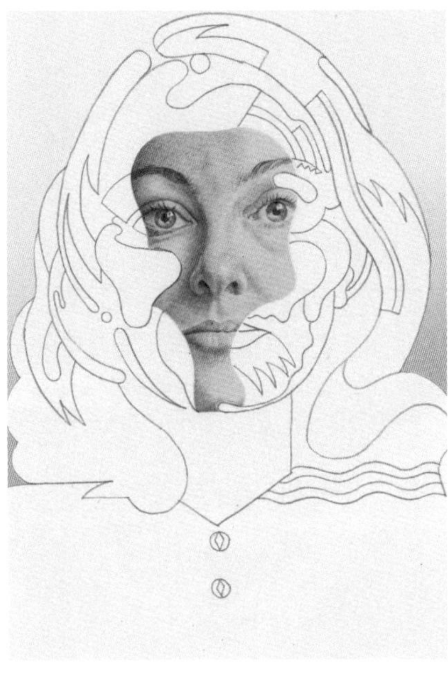

Enya Moore is a writer, editor and researcher specializing in design. Originally from Ireland, she is currently pursuing a master's degree in Design Cultures at VU University Amsterdam. A former *Frame* editor, Moore has contributed to publications such as *Icon*, *Blueprint* and the *Australian Design Review*. For *Frame* 110, she delved into the history of Hans Coray's Landi Chair.

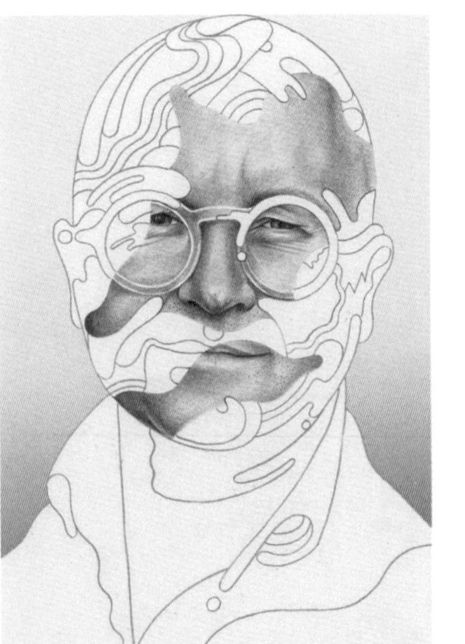

Photographer **Mikael Olsson** plies his trade in Stockholm. In 2011 he published *Södrakull Frösakull*, a book that explores the clash between man, architecture and nature in two private residences designed by Swedish architect Bruno Mathsson. Olsson is working on his next title, *On / Auf*, which is due to be released this year. For *Frame* 110, Olsson captured Note at work.

Olivier Dressen is an award-winning Belgian photographer and creative director. Although his main base is in Shanghai, Dressen also spends time in Paris, Brussels and Los Angeles. In addition to his editorial and mixed-media work, he directs commercials, short films and music videos. Dressen shot the portraits of Christina Luk of Lukstudio for this issue's rendition of 'Introducing'.

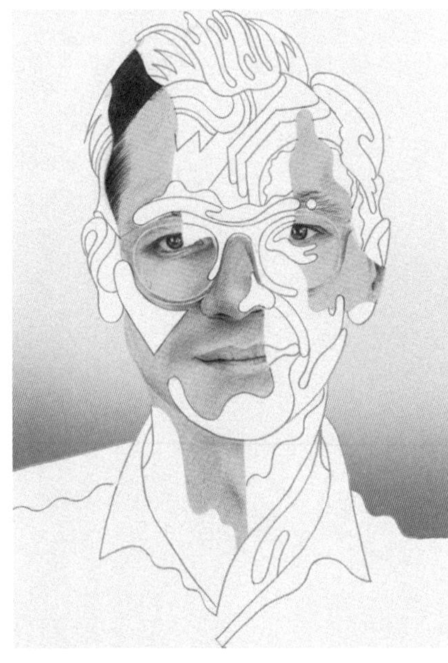

You'll find curator, writer and journalist **Daniel Golling** doing his thing in Stockholm. The former editor in chief of *Form* and *Forum*, Golling is a frequent contributor to *Mark* and other international publications, among which *Modern Design Review*, *Azure*, *Icon* and *Interni*. In 2013 he cofounded publishing house and podcast Summit. For this issue, Golling met with Swedish outfit Note.

Illustrations Sam Green

HB
led lightbar bench
www.hudsonandbroad.com

OBJECTS

Designers take *cues from cars.* Formafantasma brings *materiality to light.* Issey Miyake unfolds a *new pleated material. Classics are reborn* and *wood makes the cut* at IMM. Participants *play with processes* and *office acoustics sing out* at the Stockholm Furniture & Light Fair. All this and more is shaping the world of products.

Photo courtesy of Formafantasma

①

Watch Funt come to life with the digital magazine

Stockholm Design Week participants *experiment* with **making processes**

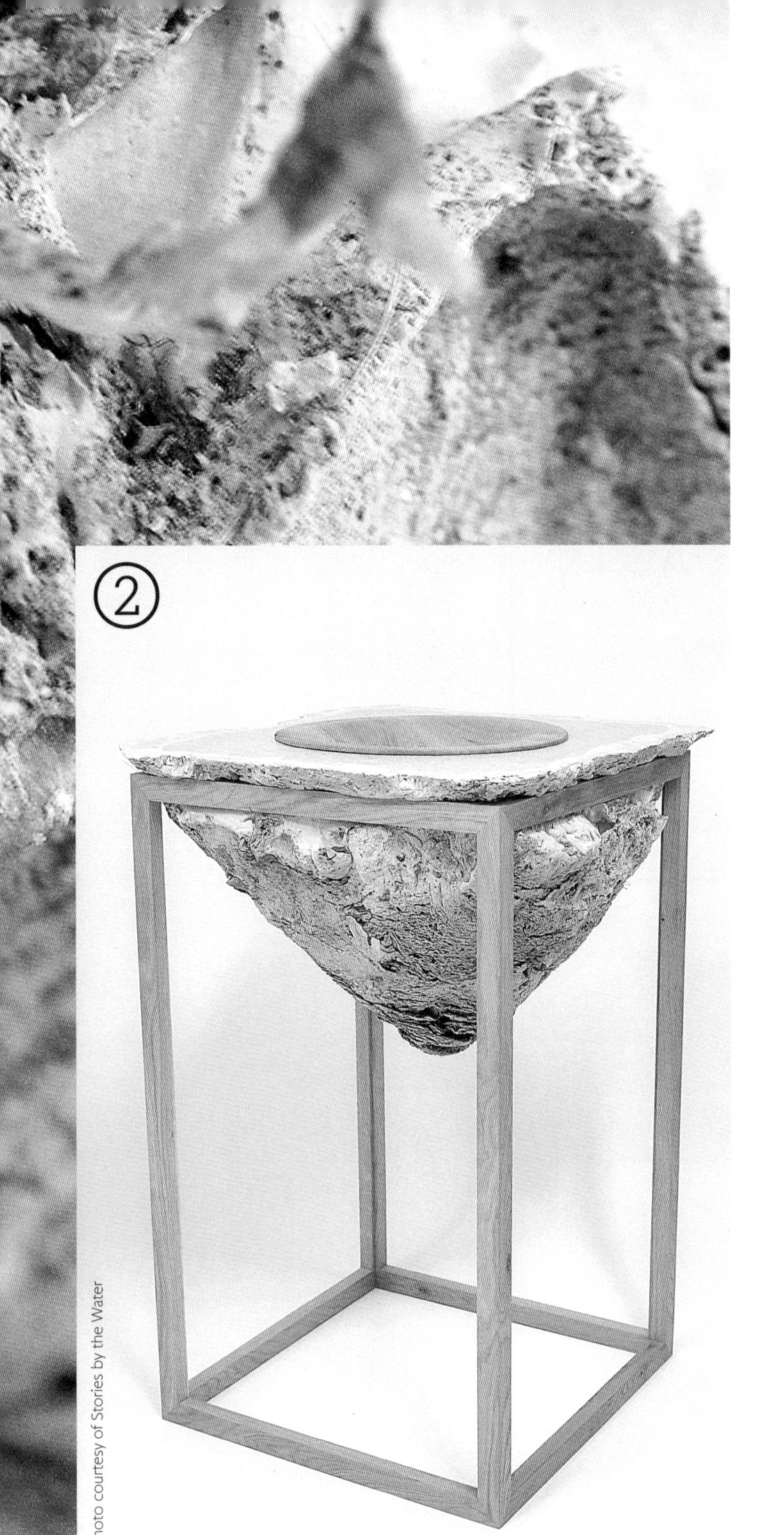

②

Photo courtesy of Stories by the Water

TREND – 'When I can imagine something, it's already there,' says Swedish-Chilean Anton Alvarez, standing in his Stockholm studio. He is explaining why he chose to leave the outcome of his latest venture at least partly up to chance. 'I design a system, not the end product,' Alvarez continues. Alphabet Aerobics, the exhibition he mounted at the National Centre for Craft & Design in Sleaford, England – the show closes on 5 June – features one of Alvarez's new machines. Using extrusion moulds with openings shaped like letters, museum staff produce one ceramic sculpture ① a day, thus removing the artist from the making process.

Work by Alvarez also appeared during Stockholm Design Week, where he was not the only contributor that made use of alternative 'shaping' techniques to obtain unique results. At the concurrent Stockholm Furniture & Light Fair, University of Gothenburg students showed Stories by the Water at the Greenhouse, a space designed by Form Us With Love. The student presentation, curated by Note Design Studio (see page 103), took Sweden's Dalsland Canal as its starting point. Among the students was Matz Engdahl, who dug a hole in the local church grounds and used it as a mould, which he filled it with liquid jesmonite. When the irregularly textured geomorphic work was dry, Engdahl turned it into a baptismal font titled Funt ②.

Studio Swine participated in the fifth edition of the Örnsbergsauktionen, which coincided with the earlier-mentioned events. For the artist-run auction house, the interdisciplinary practice known for its explorative, material-focused projects created Uo ③ (Japanese for 'fish'), an object made of recycled solid cast aluminium; a small brass shelf for displaying small objects projects from one end. To achieve Uo's dynamic one-off silhouette, the Anglo-Japanese duo employed a new method of sand-casting. – FK

antonalvarez.com
storiesbythewater.com
studioswine.com

③

Photo courtesy of Örnsbergsauktionen

Photos Frédérique Dumoulin (catwalk) / courtesy of Issey Miyake (material close-ups)

Get a feel for Issey Miyake's oven-baked garments with the digital magazine

Issey Miyake cooks up a **new recipe for pleats**

MATERIALS — Illustrious fashion designer Issey Miyake has long been associated with innovative pleating techniques. He introduced his first pleated garments in 1989, followed that same year by Pleats Please, and 1997 saw the appearance of A-Poc, which Miyake's website calls a 'manufacturing method'. In the label's S/S 2016 collection, Botanical Delights, head designer Yoshiyuki Miyamae and his team push pleats even further.

The most striking pieces – a combination of traditional Japanese methods and advanced technologies – reveal a new pleated material called Baked Stretch. When glue is imprinted onto fabric and the result is baked, the glue rises – much like bread – to fill in moulded forms that give the finished product a pattern of sinuous lines. Miyamae's process may not be immediately obvious to the customer, but the fashion house has released a poetic film that lifts the curtain on the new art of pleating. Featuring cookie-cutter-clothing manufactured on a production line, the video shows a variety of silhouettes being stamped with undulating lines of colour before going into the oven.

The brand's recent collaboration with Iittala – a range of textiles for the home – suggests that Baked Stretch may continue to move away from the catwalk and show its colours in other realms of design. — EM

isseymiyake.com

Ingredients of Marco Guazzini's *Italian identity* mix into his artisanal **alternative for marble**

MATERIALS — Marco Guazzini dives into his Mediterranean roots to find elements that represent his legacy. Woollen yarns from Prato, the Italian designer's textile-centred hometown, and waste marble collected from Pietrasanta, his holiday haven and the starting point of Michelangelo's *David*, become the main ingredients of Marwoolus, a material cocktail that solidifies his identity.

A lengthy experimentation process led to the perfect binder for uniting the dyed fibres and pulverized marble blend. Once poured into moulds, the liquid concoction enables the tufts of wool to be 'casually strewn' before hardening. He sculpts the resulting slabs as if they were quarried stone. The only detectable difference between Mother Nature's marble and the artisanal alternative? The tactility of Guazzini's rainbow-hued pigments coursing through variegated veins.

Conceived for Gallery S. Bensimon in Paris, a pair of his bespoke objects recall 8th-century Yemeni temple ruins. Sculpted from the wool-infused marble, two rows of columns rest on two rectangular plinths. Tempio del Sole, which pays homage to the solar cycle, features uprights marked by streaks of lime green, turquoise and black rising from a white base. Its darker counterpart, Tempio della Luna, worships the moon; standing on a black base, its 16 columns display a mottled motif of orange and white striae. — LG

marcoguazzini.com

Photos Beppe Brancato

At IMM, design **classics make a comeback**

Photo courtesy of Gubi

Photo courtesy of Ligne Roset

Photo courtesy of Tom Dixon

Photo courtesy of Walter Knoll

TREND — For those in the design business, the period between January and May — also known as trade-fair season — is something of a marathon. In the sprint to keep up with the latest trends, the occasional blast from the past can be surprisingly refreshing. Participating in the 'new', the 'old' proved to be an enduring source of inspiration at this year's IMM Cologne, where brands revitalized classics in a pronounced celebration of times gone by.

Ligne Roset brought back the 1980s with its curvaceous Plumy Collection ①. Reissued in collaboration with designer Annie Hiéronimus, the plump seats now feature high-performance Bultex polyurethane foam padding. Raising the comfort level of another unforgettable design was Walter Knoll, with its upholstered interpretation of the Fishnet Chair ②. The work of Sadi & Neptun Ozis, the 1959 edition consisted of little more than a web of thread. Today it flaunts a fuller form. Meanwhile, Britain's Tom Dixon reconsidered a 17th-century staple: the Wingback Chair ③. The dramatic proportions he applied to the archetypal silhouette elevate the status of

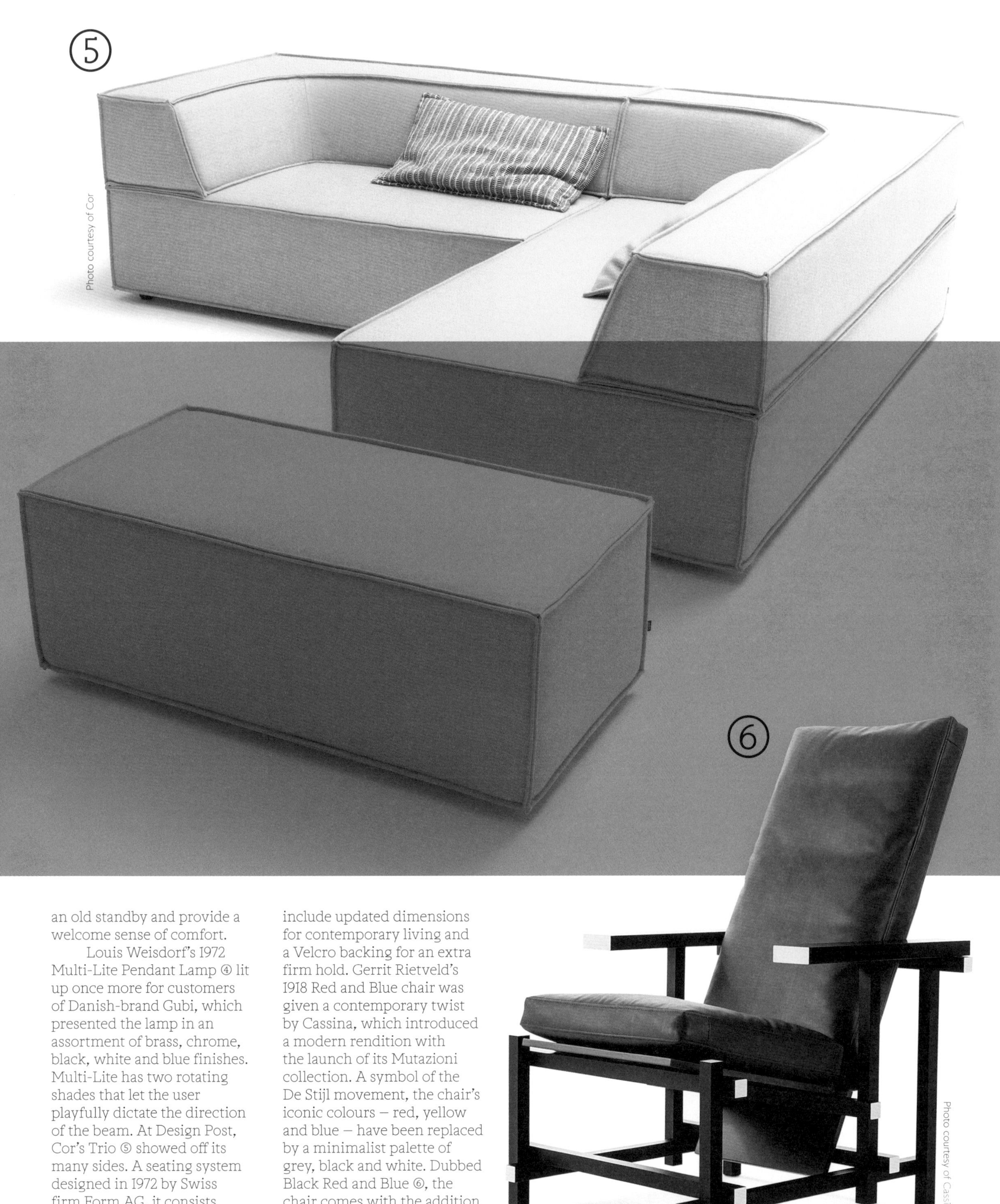

Photo courtesy of Cor

an old standby and provide a welcome sense of comfort.

Louis Weisdorf's 1972 Multi-Lite Pendant Lamp ④ lit up once more for customers of Danish-brand Gubi, which presented the lamp in an assortment of brass, chrome, black, white and blue finishes. Multi-Lite has two rotating shades that let the user playfully dictate the direction of the beam. At Design Post, Cor's Trio ⑤ showed off its many sides. A seating system designed in 1972 by Swiss firm Form AG, it consists of a series of 13 elements. Improvements to the original include updated dimensions for contemporary living and a Velcro backing for an extra firm hold. Gerrit Rietveld's 1918 Red and Blue chair was given a contemporary twist by Cassina, which introduced a modern rendition with the launch of its Mutazioni collection. A symbol of the De Stijl movement, the chair's iconic colours – red, yellow and blue – have been replaced by a minimalist palette of grey, black and white. Dubbed Black Red and Blue ⑥, the chair comes with the addition of a padded seat and backrest cushions. – MEO

Photo courtesy of Cassina

Maarten Baas opts for **metal patchwork** in his *new collection*

FURNITURE — Carapace, a line of furniture by Dutch designer Maarten Baas, is appearing in New York City at Carpenters Workshop Gallery (until 30 April). Occupying the gallery's newly opened exhibition space, the six-piece collection is hard to miss. Each item is defined by an organized chaos of spot-welded bronze or steel patchwork, a look that resembles the exoskeleton or 'carapace' of creatures like beetles, crabs and turtles. 'The works explore the feeling of vulnerability,' says Baas, that opposes 'the desire for development in the environment'. His words express the design of furniture whose tough outer shield protects a softer interior, such as an armchair featuring alpaca-wool upholstery and a cupboard lined in warm walnut. — LM

maartenbaas.com

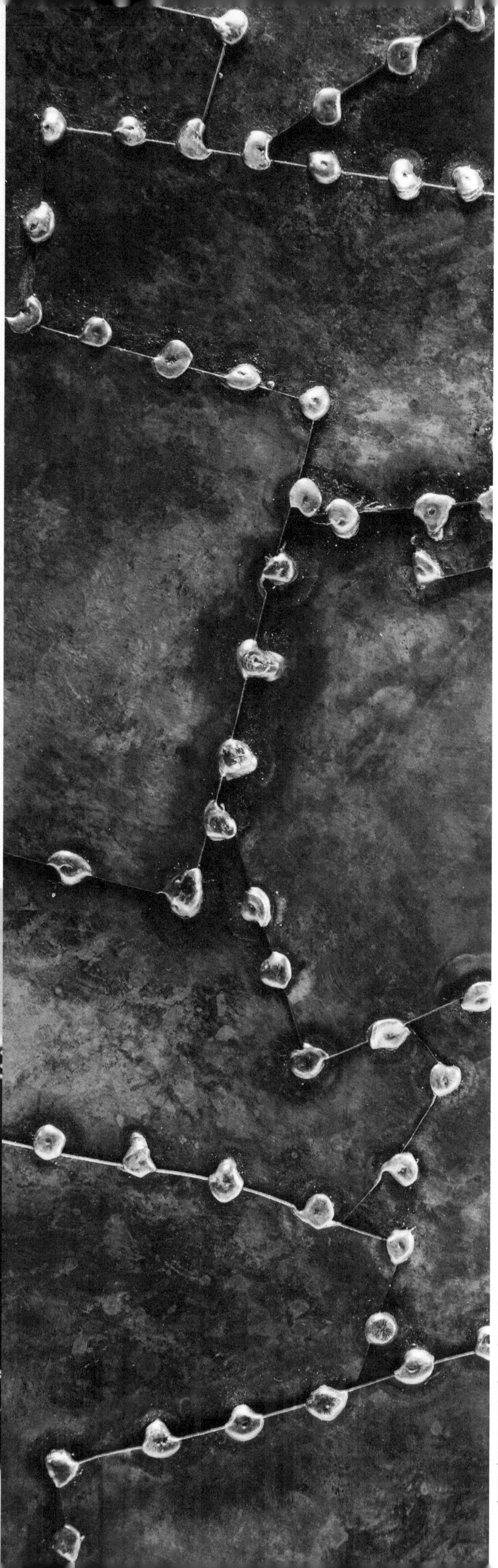

Photos Adrien Millot, courtesy of Carpenters Workshop Gallery

Car culture prompts designers and makers to appropriate **automotive aesthetics**

TREND – The automotive industry is a frontrunner in the field of innovative design, and its tech-savvy solutions haven't gone unnoticed by those in other creative disciplines. As a result, we are seeing an increasing amount of cross-pollination, as exemplified by car brand Tesla's expansion into the energy scene and the use of embroidery techniques developed by car manufacturers turning up in high-performance footwear by multinationals like Adidas. But it's not just automotive technology that's informing fashion and product design. From classic cars to the curves of Formula 1's latest models, designers are looking to automobiles for aerodynamic shapes, intricate parts and gleaming finishes – on multiple levels. Need a ride? – FK

Photo courtesy of Christopher Kane

1 Drawing upon Japan's rich car culture, Chris Labrooy shot a computer-generated series of images in Tokyo; the photos feature the Honda NSX, the Toyota AE86 and two Datsun models: 240Z and Skyline GTR.

2 Inspired by automobile assemblages by John Chamberlain, Christopher Kane's F/W 2016 menswear collection reflects 'the streets'.

3 For Exaptation Composition N°5, ÉCAL graduate Maxime Guyon applied glossy digital prints of car close-ups to bent steel plates. Some images are manipulated.

4 Fool's Gold – a cabinet and console by Lanzavecchia + Wai – is constructed out of corrugated steel and finished with a gold-chrome car wrap.

5 German Unibro Design transformed automotive parts into a furniture collection that includes a Mustang car-bonnet desk and a standing lamp topped with an engine filter.

6 Supporting the launch of its Q30 model, automotive brand Infiniti developed the Seeker, a GPS-enabled compass.

GRAND PUBLIC
LAMMHULTS
WE WILL ALWAYS BE MODERN, OUR DESIGN ALWAYS ESSENTIAL

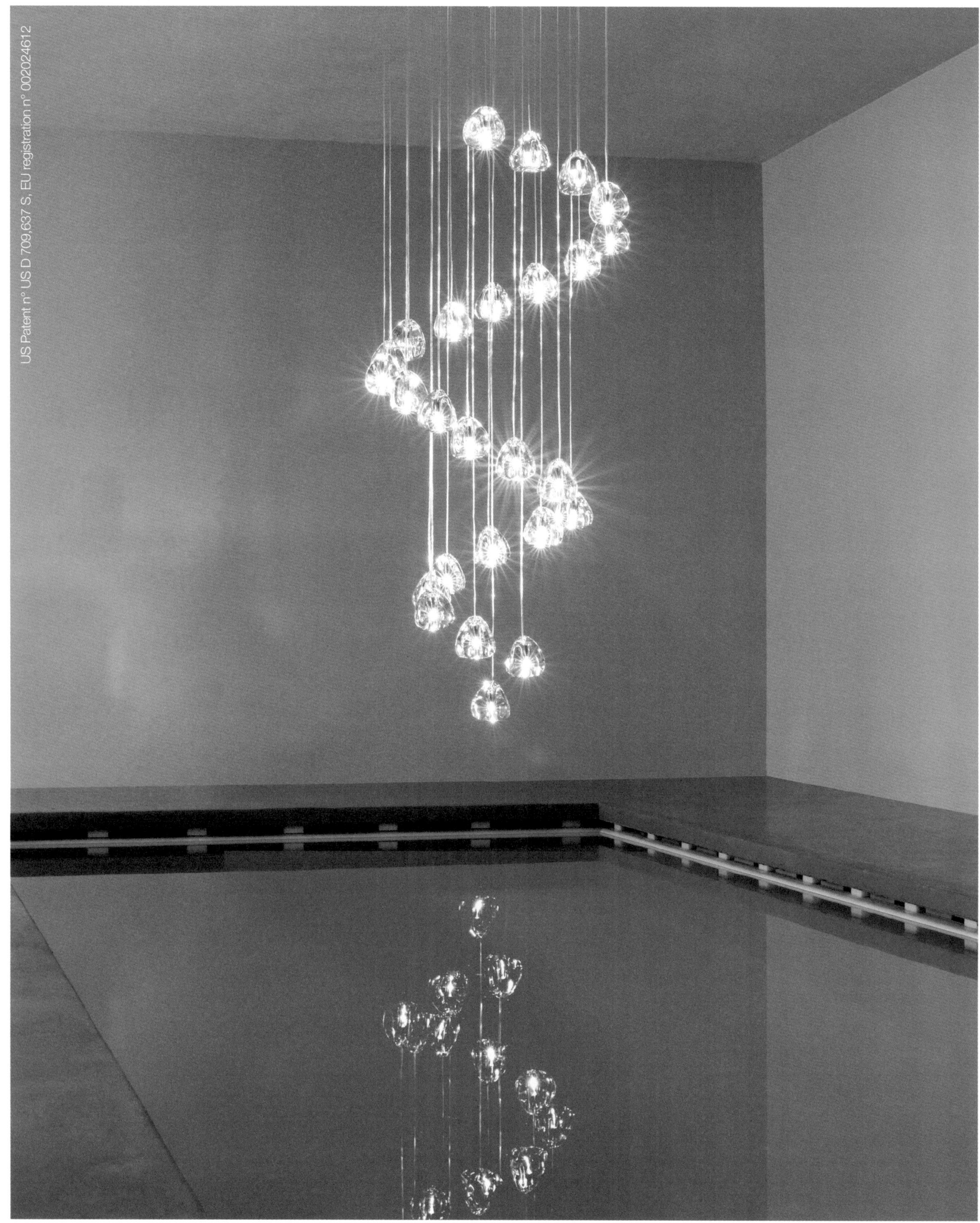
US Patent n° US D 709,637 S, EU registration n° 002024612
terzani.com
Mizu, Flowing Light
design Nicolas Terzani
TERZANI
LA LUCE PENSATA

Timber takes a stand at IMM

FURNITURE — We can pretend all we want, but nothing quite compares to the look and feel of good old-fashioned natural wood. Throughout the halls of IMM Cologne, it was hard not to notice the swell of sylvan wonders.

Thonet's 1060 dining table ① turned heads with its slender silhouette and provocative V-shaped legs. Made from solid bentwood, two round members on opposite ends split into three to form the table's base and legs. A design by Dutchman Jorre van Ast, 1060 is available in oak and ash, either stained or lacquered. An additional walnut version features a contrasting frame available with a black- or white-painted finish.

Ton introduced its minimalist Moon armchair ②. Marrying craft with comfort, Ton's Moon has an upholstered seat and backrest accented by slender armrests that appear to embrace the chair from the rear. The sober seats are the work of Slovak designer Michal Riabič.

Sharing with Ton an apparent affinity for the extraterrestrial, Living Divani presented Moon ③. Part side table, part storage unit, the design by Japanese-Italian studio Mist-o comprises two half-circles that meet at its centre to form a perfect sphere. When separated, the twin components reveal a structured interior for storing books and other small objects.

'Wood is an elementary material. It has longevity,' says German designer Mathias Hahn, who together with Zeitraum celebrated the launch of the brand's solid-wood storage system, Kin ④. A family of modular cabinets, the collection consists of six individual elements. Designed to adapt to changing environments, the cabinets can stand alone or be combined to form any number of quirky compositions.

For his sixth design for French furniture brand Hartô, Pierre-François Dubois turned to the seas. Inspired by the hull and sails of a ship, the Marius ⑤ sideboard is characterized by a gently curved base and delicate markings that run diagonally across the front of the piece to form a rhythmic pattern. – MEO

③

Photo courtesy of Living Divani

④

Photo courtesy of Zeitraum

Photo courtesy of Thonet

Photo courtesy of Ton

②

⑤

Photo courtesy of Hartô

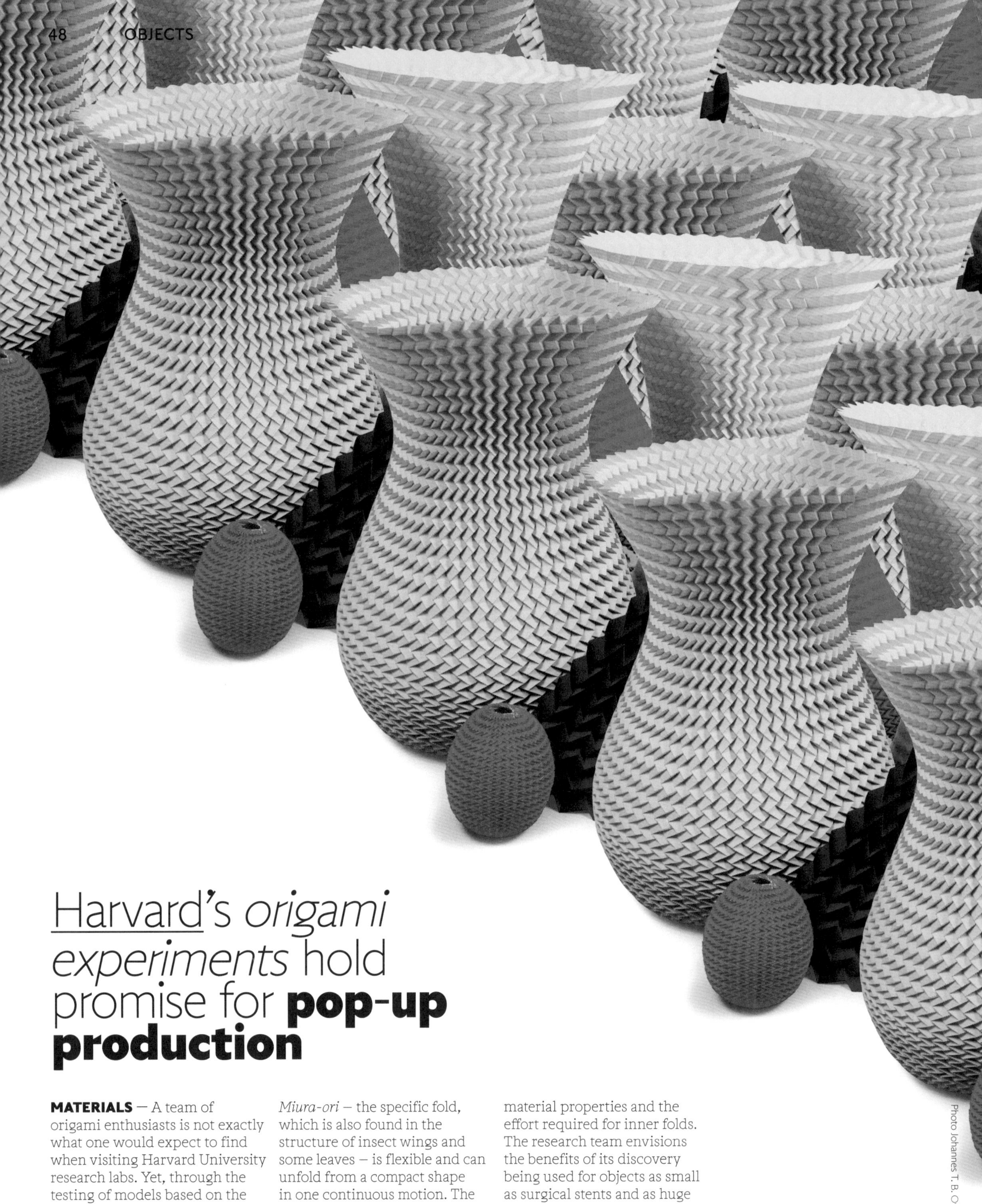

Harvard's *origami experiments* hold promise for **pop-up production**

MATERIALS — A team of origami enthusiasts is not exactly what one would expect to find when visiting Harvard University research labs. Yet, through the testing of models based on the traditional Japanese paper-folding technique, Professor L. Mahadevan and his team have singled out a core origami fold with the potential to act as a building block in the creation of countless numbers of 3D shapes. *Miura-ori* — the specific fold, which is also found in the structure of insect wings and some leaves — is flexible and can unfold from a compact shape in one continuous motion. The investigation has resulted in an algorithm for the tailoring of origami patterns that can be laser-printed onto various materials and applied at any scale, while also accounting for contributing elements such as material properties and the effort required for inner folds. The research team envisions the benefits of its discovery being used for objects as small as surgical stents and as huge as skyscrapers. — EM

seas.harvard.edu

Photo Johannes T. B. Overvelde, Mahadevan Group

Stockholm Furniture & Light Fair *exhibitors* give ear to **office acoustics**

TREND – As reported in *Frame* 108, which featured a work-themed Frame Lab, the open-plan office is winning terrain (again). But the setup – despite the fact that it stimulates communication and interaction – comes with a slew of design challenges. Within today's bustling workplace, acoustics are key: a subject tackled by more than one company at this year's Stockholm Furniture & Light Fair.

As part of its Lab collection, Offecct presented Wind ①, a series of nature-inspired room dividers by Jin Kuramoto, who says they function spatially 'like a kind of tuner'. Swedese extended the Gap sofa system with Gap Meeting ②, which has high side and back panels and functions as a 'room within a room'. Scala ③, a design by Anya Sebton for Abstracta, takes cues from corrugated iron. The sound-absorbing panels can be mounted on wall or ceiling to achieve 'a softer soundscape'.

The Portus range ④ from Lammhults includes easy chairs, stools and sofas for two or three persons. Backrests come in two heights and are curved; the wings of the taller chairs block noise on both sides, providing excellent acoustic privacy. Peter Hiort-Lorenzen and Johannes Foersom are responsible for the design. Baux introduced Plank ⑤. Developed to dampen noise, Plank acoustic panels – the work of Form Us With Love – expand the brand's tile collection with a customizable product that is easy to install. Last but not least, the pieces in Olle Gyllang's modular series Fields ⑥, designed for Kinnarps, adapt to virtually any working environment. Users can combine sofas, tables, screens and easy chairs to create areas for everything from socializing to complete concentration. – FK

Photo Mårten Ryner

Photo courtesy of Swedese

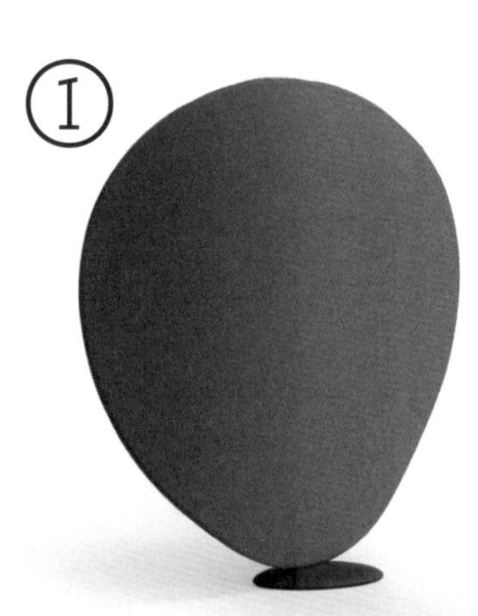

Photo Thomas Harrysson, courtesy of Offecct AB

⑤
⑥
④
Photo courtesy of Kinnarps
Photo Pelle Wahlgren
Photo courtesy of Baux AB

Vitra's *library of colours and materials* promises to be a **supportive tool** for interior design

COLOUR – 'I can't do it as a stylist. I've got to do it as a designer, as an auteur,' was Hella Jongerius's reply when Vitra's Rolf Fehlbaum asked her to revisit the brand's spectrum of colours. And the Dutch designer did just that. Following in the footsteps of notables like Alexander Girard, who also worked on vividly coloured textiles with the likes of Herman Miller and the Eameses, Jongerius set out to compile Vitra's use of colours and materials in a 'library'. A decade into her collaboration with the Swiss company, the library is ready to be used as a tool, and the joint venture is ready for a wrap-up. The wrap-up takes the shape of a book, *I Don't Have a Favourite Colour: Creating the Vitra Colour & Material Library*, released during Milan Design Week.

Here, too, the auteurism of colour plays a key role. From Jean Prouvé's saturated metals to the icy blues of Jasper Morrison, the publication includes multiple designer-specific colour wheels, finally brought together in a comprehensive system – the ultimate wheel – which serves as an intelligent library of colours and materials. Jongerius believes this library can be a helpful tool for consumers *and* professionals. It's a highly functional system that includes a changing number of so-called bridge colours (12 at this time), which are available in all materials and which make it easy for an interior designer to create a cohesively composed palette. Other, more 'exclusive', colours are part of the scheme as well. 'That's ingrained in the system,' says Jongerius. 'We isolate certain colours for temporary use by specific designers. We call them "signature colours".'

To present the tool at Milan's Fuorisalone, Jongerius – in her role as Vitra's art director for colours and materials – worked with Bas van Tol to create Colour Machine, an installation of spinning wheels made up of fragments from Vitra's furniture collection. Colours are – you guessed it – from the library's colour wheels. – FK

vitra.com

Photo Labadie van Tol, courtesy of Vitra

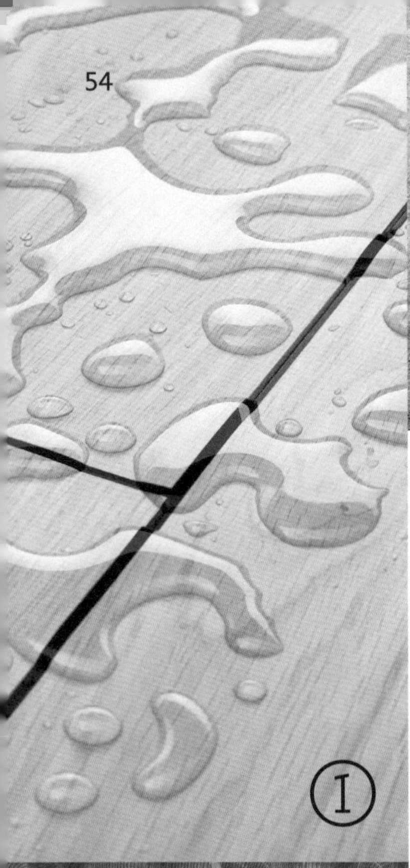

1

3

5

6

7

2

4

Floors **get smart** at Domotex

FLOORING – Surfaces underfoot are smarter than we think – or so the exhibitors at Hannover's Domotex would have us believe. Among the novelties paving the way this year – in soft, hard, wood and resilient flooring – are easy-to-install systems, super-natural finishes, and mix-and-match aesthetics. – MEO

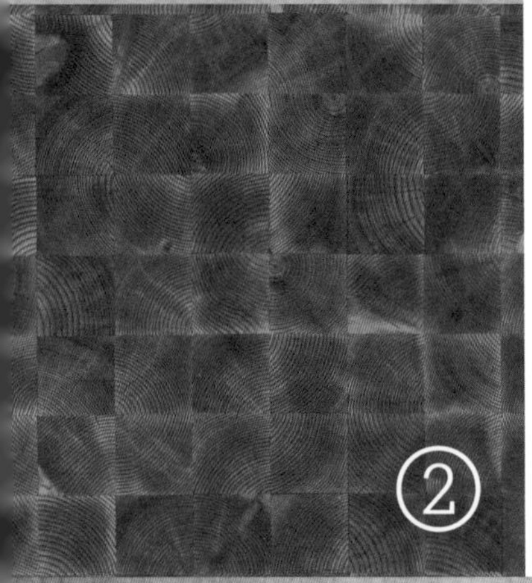

1 Intended for wet areas, Hüma's Hydro Parquet is made from real wood, which may seem to be a counterintuitive material for bathrooms and showers, but waterproof rubber joints come to the rescue. Besides being an eco-friendly choice, Hydro Parquet is easy to lay and doesn't require gluing, sanding or varnishing.

2 Made of 40-x-40-mm crosscut timber blocks – in larch or ash – Domino from Austrian company Mafi boasts a series of striking patterns. The floor is thermally treated without the use of chemical additives, making it not only robust but also 100 per cent natural.

3 Pixel, a lively carpet tile from Balta Group's Modulyss, comes in six colourways and is compatible with the brand's Patchwork and Pattern collections.

4 The extra-large vinyl tiles and planks in Beaulieu's Pure collection are a cinch to install, thanks to the brand's DreamClick locking system. Available in wood, stone and solid-colour finishes, the products are extremely lightweight and 100 per cent waterproof.

5 The antimicrobial silver ions in T-Pure – an optional finish from Swiss brand Tisca Tiara – are responsible for the elimination of odours and for a nearly total reduction of the bacteria on carpets and textiles to which it is applied. T-Pure is hygienic and environmentally sound.

6 Featuring the company's flexible Unifit locking system, Project Floors' Click Collection snaps in and out of place for quick installation. Depending on the situation, Click Collection planks – available in wood and stone finishes – can be laid linearly or at an angle.

7 Moduleo, a brand belonging to the IVC Group, adds a dose of creativity to vinyl flooring with its Moduleo Moods collection. Available in wood and stone finishes, the range includes a myriad of shapes – herringbone, chevron, triangle, rectangle, diamond – which combine to make up to 110 intricate motifs.

8 A design by Patricia Urquiola, Listone Giordano's playful Biscuit parquet comes in six formats. Marked by their distinctive shapes and sizes, the planks fit together like a puzzle. Rounded ends and bevelled edges allow users to mix and match to their hearts' content.

9 A choice of medium or large planks, which can be laid parallel or at right angles to each other, make up Bauwerk Parquet's simple yet sophisticated Formpark series. A design by Zurich's Studio Hannes Wettstein, the system features a subtle play of surface and light.

10 The flexible Squeeze rug, designed and made by Sweden's Studio Brieditis & Evans, is hand-knitted using leftover T-shirt material from India's textile industry. The fabric's double-knit structure provides Squeeze with excellent elastic properties. Measuring approximately 90 × 400 cm, the runner manoeuvres comfortably around tight corners.

11 LooseLay from Designflooring has a 'friction-grip backing' that secures the product to the subfloor without the use of adhesives. The hard-wearing, low-maintenance vinyl floor covering is available in wood, stone and concrete finishes and as tiles or planks. Easy on both eyes and feet, LooseLay cushioned planks also provide good acoustic insulation.

12 Designed to look like broadloom, ZigZag-Tiles from Fletco offer the practical advantages of a modular system: a damaged tile can be removed and replaced in a flash. Wavy edges on two sides of each tile are laser cut to guarantee a perfect fit and a smooth surface.

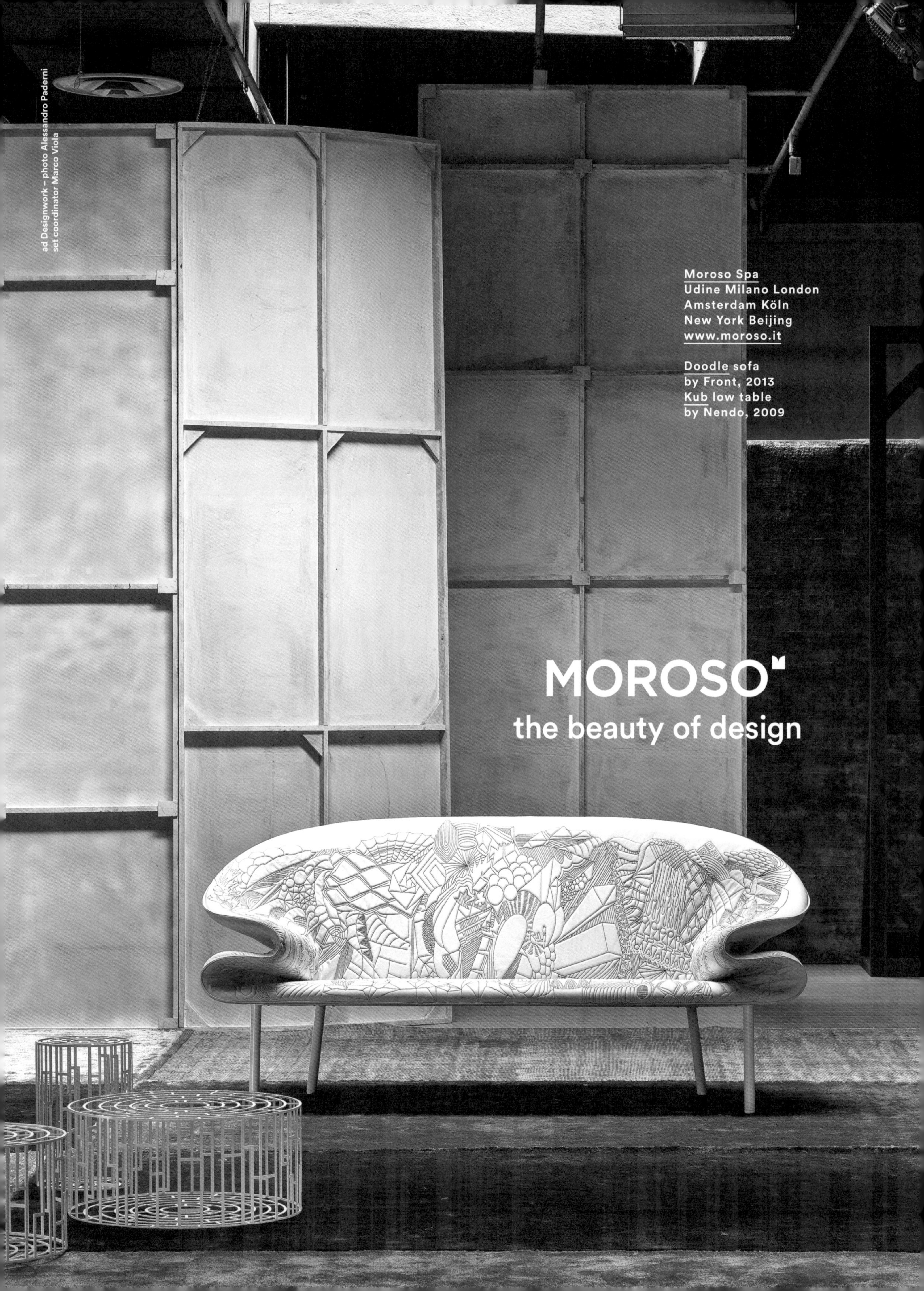

Photos courtesy of Formafantasma

Formafantasma explores the **materiality of light**

LIGHTING — While Andrea Trimarchi and Simone Farresin of Studio Formafantasma are most often celebrated for their craftsmanship, the objects on display at Milan's Peep-Hole gallery demonstrate a slight shift towards a more industrial approach. For their Anno Tropico exhibition, the Italian duo employed light ingeniously paired with tactile counterparts, such as bronze and concrete, while exploiting the reflective possibilities of light to dramatic effect. Accompanying drawings, models and a video explain the process behind the investigation and elaborate on the experimental nature of the Amsterdam-based practice. Light represents not only the theme of the show but also its schedule, as opening hours vary according to the changing light of day. – EM

formafantasma.com

The properties of natural light are revealed in the digital magazine

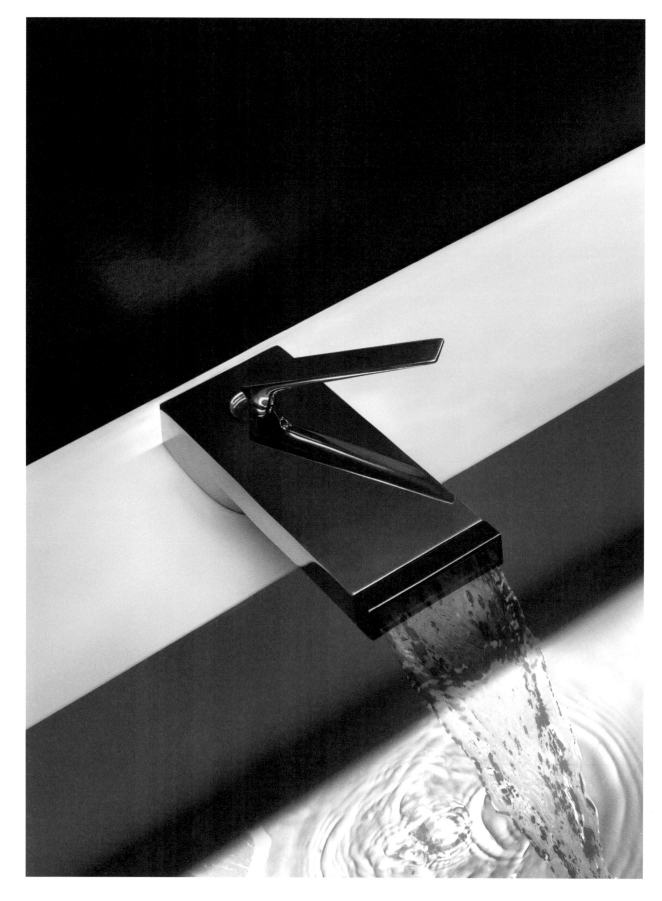

TALENTS

Aurelie Hoegy puts the *'extra' in extraordinary*. Studio Brynjar & Veronika thrives on *nature*. Yuri Suzuki plays with the *power of sound*. Meet our curated selection of award-winning creatives.

Photo Fabrice Gousset

Sound Artist **Yuri Suzuki**

In tune with his urban surroundings, a London-based Japanese musician stresses the power of sound.

Photo Dentaku

Designed together with Mark McKeague, Naomi Eliott and Joseph Pleass, Yuri Suzuki's Ototo is a pocket-sized electronic DJ set. Flexible crocodile clips attach a miniature PSB synthesizer to conductive materials to generate sound.

How would you describe your work? YURI SUZUKI: I use sound as a material. My work is multidisciplinary; it intersects with many fields, such as technology, interactive and product design, installation art and film. Basically, my work is anything that involves or can be used to create sound.

What inspires you? Music mostly, but also sound in general. The 'music' that surrounds us daily.

Is your work influenced by any particular movement or person? I'm influenced by a wide variety of fields and people. Just a few of those that come to mind – many of whom I had the fortune to work with or study under – are Alexander Calder, Christian Marclay, Maywa Denki, Jeff Mills, Radiophonic Workshop, Kraftwerk, Tim Hunkin, Durrell Bishop, Jesper Kouthoofd, Anthony Dunne, Åbäke, Takeshi Ishiguro and DMX Krew.

Are there projects you'd like to work on that haven't yet come your way? I'd like to get back to doing sound installations. My last solo show was in 2010, so it's been a while. I'd like to develop my personal work a bit more. More recently, I've been getting into performance projects and developing work related to music and children's education, which I really enjoy. I'd like to continue working in this field. I've also thought about developing new musical instruments and directing music videos.

Describe your creative process in five words. Dream, try, fail, dream, and try. Then repeat the sequence.

Where do you think design is headed? In the past, design was about improving the way people live. I think design today is focused too heavily on the business side of things. There's nothing wrong with business, but there needs to be a balance. — MEO

yurisuzuki.com

RECIPIENT OF THE 2016 SWAROVSKI DESIGNERS OF THE FUTURE AWARD

KFF
KIRK ALUMINIUM AND FINEST LEATHER
WWW.KFF.DE

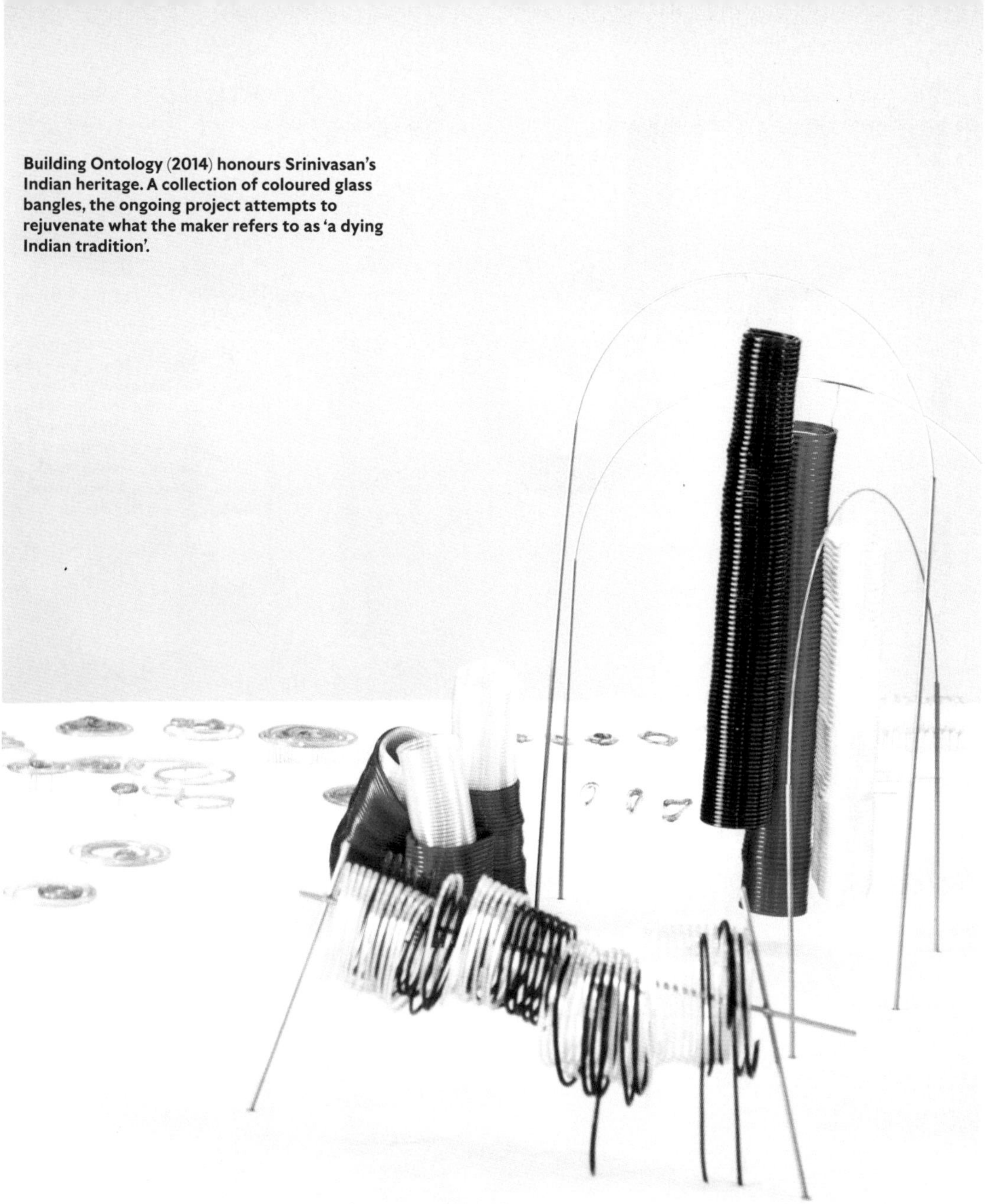

Building Ontology (2014) honours Srinivasan's Indian heritage. A collection of coloured glass bangles, the ongoing project attempts to rejuvenate what the maker refers to as 'a dying Indian tradition'.

Artist **Anjali Srinivasan**

Mindful of her Indian heritage, a glass-maker in Dubai marries past and present in her work.

Tell me about your work. ANJALI SRINIVASAN: My work varies with each project, ranging from the design of humble tools to the realization of spectacular installations. Lately I have been working on objects and forms that can grow, expand and mutate continuously over time.

Where do you find inspiration? In life. Our days are packed with an immeasurable number of beautiful, fleeting moments. Whether it's being delighted by a taste or disturbed by a sensation, I believe every minute of every day has the potential to feed creativity.

What are you proudest of? The very thing I feel most uncomfortable about: the fact that I'm an artist. By 'artist', I mean someone who is able to approach the world in an unexpected way, someone whose hands can transform questions and thoughts into objects and experiences.

Where do you think design is going? I don't think a single statement would be fair here. Each culture has its own ideas about design, and I couldn't possibly claim familiarity with all of them. What I *can* tell you, however, is where I'd *like* to see design headed. I hope design will become more human-centred. I'd like to see fewer gimmicks and more thoughtfulness. I want to see designs that merge old and new technologies, ones that are both environmentally and culturally sustainable and that add value to human interactions, lift spirits and inform new ways of thinking and making. I believe design should be approached from the perspective of the object. If the object could speak, what would it say? — MEO

anjalisrinivasan.com

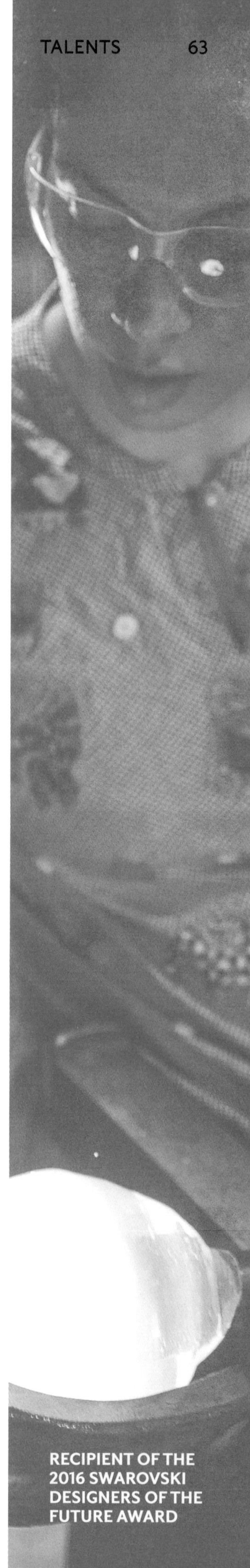

RECIPIENT OF THE 2016 SWAROVSKI DESIGNERS OF THE FUTURE AWARD

Silent Village, a collection of whimsical furniture designed for Galerie Kreo in Paris, pays homage to Brynjar Sigurðarson's encounters in a small Icelandic fishing town.

Photo Fabrice Gousset

Product Designers **Studio Brynjar & Veronika**

When it comes to drawing inspiration from nature, two Berlin-based designers go the distance.

Can you describe your work? VERONIKA SEDLMAIR: We try to follow our intuition and to trust our senses. We work a lot with nature, so being close to and engaging with the environment is important to us. We enjoy stepping outside our comfort zone and exploring different creative fields, such as art and music. Paradoxically, it's where we feel most at ease.

Are you influenced by any particular movement or person? What inspires us most are people who are passionate about what they are doing. Besides trying to surround ourselves with enthusiastic people, we look to nearby sources – the city and nature – for inspiration. Brynjar [Sigurðarson], who is from Iceland, is deeply influenced by the natural world. The Icelandic landscape informs much of our work.

What's your dream project? We'd love to have the chance to collaborate with dancers, actors and musicians – or to work on a project that combines the different performance arts. Designing and building a summer house or cabin in Iceland is also high on the list. We've also thought about making a movie one day. These are only a few on our very long list.

What is one thing you can't live without? We lead ourselves to believe that we can't live without certain objects, when in fact that's not the case. If we had to pick one thing, though, it would probably be our computers. That said, we would love to try to live without them one day.

What does your workspace or studio look like? Lately, we've been working out of our home. It's a nice space, but it poses some challenges, particularly when it comes to experimenting with materials and models. Things can get complicated and messy rather quickly. — MEO

biano.is

RECIPIENT OF THE 2016 SWAROVSKI DESIGNERS OF THE FUTURE AWARD

FLORIM
ELEGANCE
EVERYDAY ELEGANCE
The ability to choose is a way of life.
Elegance is not innate, rather it is choice:
Rex offers precious collections of
fine porcelain stoneware inspired by
the nature of noble materials.
Refined colors blend with exclusive
graphics solutions available in amazing sizes.
FLORIM OVERSIZE
magnum
160x320
120x240
80x240
26,5x240
160x160
120x120
www.florim.it
collections: pietra del nord nero - statuario glossy
rex
CERAMICHE ARTISTICHE
MADE IN FLORIM

WINNER OF MOMA PS1'S 2016 YOUNG ARCHITECTS PROGRAM

Architects **Escobedo Soliz Studio**

Experimental Mexican architects weave new worlds that enhance existing spaces.

Image Pedro Lechuga-Cuervo Loco, courtesy of Escobedo Soliz Studio

Weaving the Courtyard is a site-specific architectural installation set to open in June at MoMA PS1. The project consists of an artificial landscape, a paddling pool and a chromatic canopy, or 'cloud' of crisscrossing ropes.

Tell me a bit about your work. ANDRÉS SOLIZ PAZ: Our work is a constant investigation of the elements that create space, such as light and matter. We try to work with the pre-existing conditions of each project, from the topography to the people and their traditions. It's an intuitive process. We start by engaging with the site, exchanging ideas about what we see and making sketches. These encounters and impressions are what eventually lead to our first models.

What inspires you? Inspiration can come from anywhere. All it takes is a bit of observation. Besides architecture, we often look to other creative disciplines and to everyday objects for inspiration.

Who are your influences? There are a handful of architecture 'masters' that we admire – people like Louis Kahn, Alvar Aalto, Luis Barragán, Sverre Fehn, Peter Zumthor, Dom Hans van der Laan and Aldo van Eyck, to name but a few. During our studies, Humberto Ricalde and Gabriela Carrillo influenced us greatly. They still inspire us today.

What would be your dream project site? We would like to work on projects in our hometowns. Pavel is from Nayarit, a beautiful state on the Pacific coast of Mexico, and my family comes from Cochabamba, a little city in Bolivia. We not only have strong ties to these places; we also think they have a lot of potential.

Describe your creative process in five words. Observe, imagine, experiment, discover and polish.

What do you envision for the future of design? It's hard to say. There are so many things happening right now in the industry: things we aren't even aware of. The speed at which design – as well as life in general – is moving has changed a lot. We don't think too much about it, though. We prefer to focus on our practice, which is the only thing that we can more or less control. — MEO

escobedosoliz.net

Designer **Aurelie Hoegy**

A French artist and designer puts the 'extra' into extraordinary objects.

How would you describe your work? AURELIE HOEGY: My work is where the ordinary and the absurd converge. It questions reality and breaks barriers between normality and abnormality, between gesture and object. I want to draw people out of the known universe, with its customs and rituals, and into a foreign dimension.

Is your work influenced by any particular styles? I am constantly trying to merge my work with different disciplines, such as film, dance, theatre and music. My Macguffin lamp, for instance, takes its cue from plot devices and other cinematographic methods used by cult directors such as Alfred Hitchcock, David Lynch and Jacques Tati. I'm interested in the way in which their films shift our perception of the everyday. To me, cinema is similar to design in that they both have the potential to generate alternative realities. Recently I have been looking to contemporary dance, and in particular the choreography of William Forsythe, for inspiration.

Tell me about your ideal project. I would like to work with filmmakers and fashion designers. I find the idea of designing costumes and objects for a fantastical universe very enticing. I'm always keen to work on projects that disturb reality and push the imagination.

Describe your workspace. Picture a cabin on a mezzanine with huge windows overlooking a theatre, with people coming and going, lugging props and other things around. Eight of us share the space, which is filled with all sorts of experiments. Most of the others work in film or as set designers. We make pieces for my Dancers collection upstairs. It can be a bit scary up there, with all the latex, cords and threads hanging about.

Define your creative process in five words. Observation, thought, action, struggle, action. — MEO

aureliehoegy.com

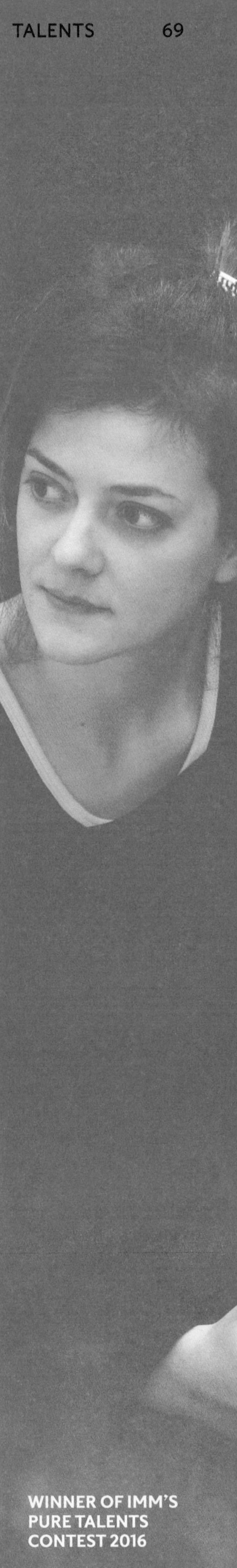

WINNER OF IMM'S PURE TALENTS CONTEST 2016

Hybrids of seating and sculpture, pieces in Hoegy's Dancers collection question the functionality of design by 'disturbing' its prime model: the chair.

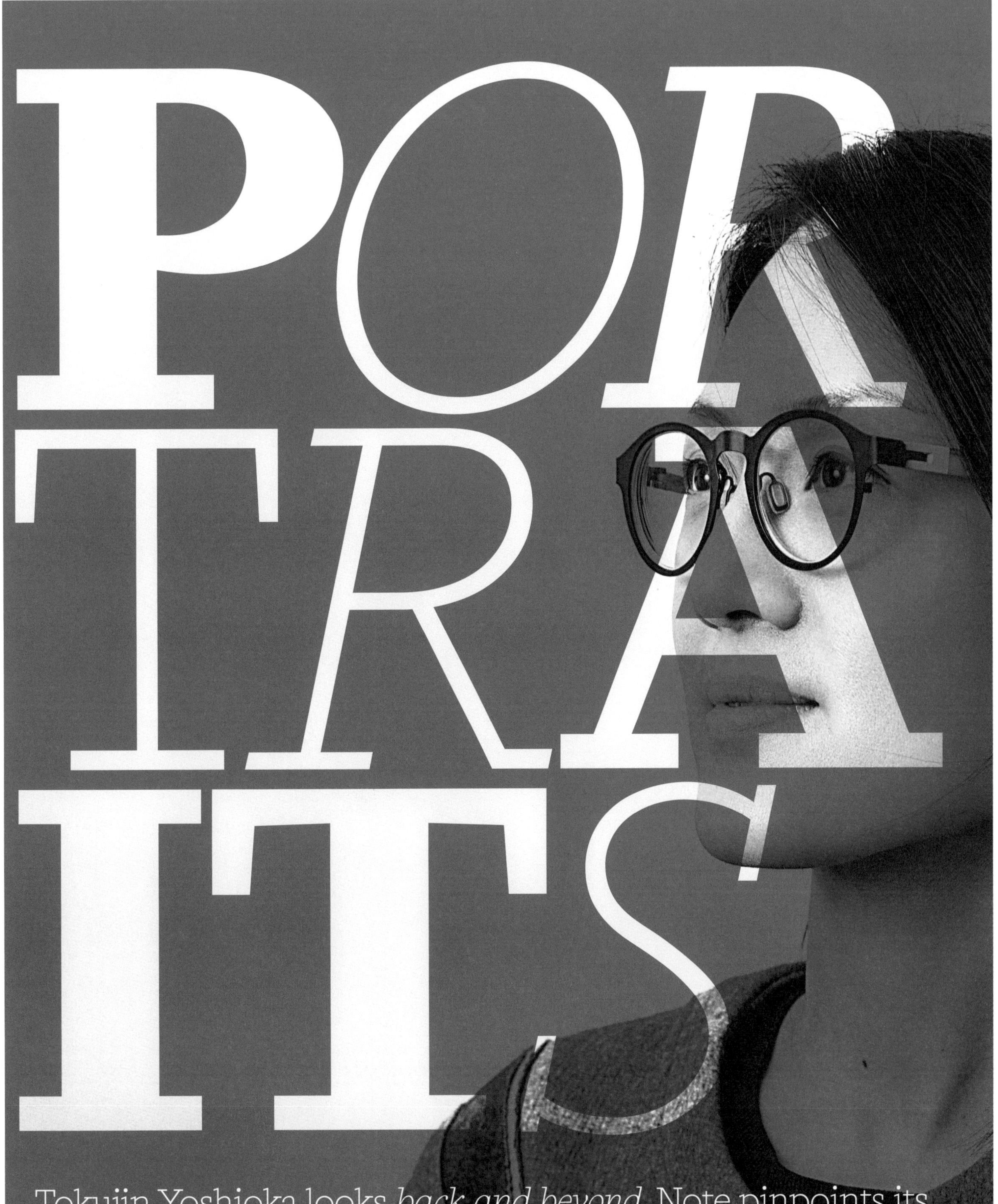

PORTRAITS

Tokujin Yoshioka looks *back and beyond*. Note pinpoints its *landmark projects*. Lukstudio sets up a *springboard in Shanghai*. Chiharu Shiota *strings together space*. Marieke and Pieter Sanders put their *design collection* to use. Doshi Levien *diarizes a day*. Get all this and even more *perspectives on people*.

Photo Olivier H. Dressen

Well **Versed**

Approaching 50 years of age, Tokujin Yoshioka reflects on a *life dedicated to producing poetic designs.*

Words **Kanae Hasegawa** Portraits **Tada** (**Yukai**)

Tokujin Yoshioka

1967 Born in Saga Prefecture, Japan

1986 Graduates from Kuwasawa Design School, Tokyo, Japan
Works under Shiro Kuramata and Issey Miyake

2000 Opens own studio, Tokujin Yoshioka Inc., in Tokyo

2001 Shows paper chair Honey-Pop at Milan Design Week

2006 Releases Pane, a polyester-elastomer chair without an inner frame

2015 Realizes Kou-An Glass Tea House

TOKUJIN YOSHIOKA: 'I was brought up in a region called Saga. It's part of Kyushu Island, the most southwestern of Japan's four main islands. I spent my childhood in an environment far removed from the design world and the material cultures found in metropolises. If I had a pencil in my hand, I would get swept up in drawing.'

'I was absorbed by the art and science classes at school. At a young age, I was thrilled to discover that when you draw on paper with citrus juice and then apply heat, colour appears on the paper – it's like something a spy uses to send coded messages. Exploring how to manipulate such natural phenomena fascinated me. It gave me great delight to see my classmates mesmerized by what I was doing; that's the reason I was driven to continue making things that people enjoy. Besides that, I was a quiet boy.'

'When I was young, I couldn't imagine there being such a profession as *designer*. Back then, I associated the word with fashion designers, not furniture designers. I didn't think it was possible to make a living out of drawing and making things – activities that gave me pure joy.'

"I always try to create something that doesn't yet exist

'I went to Kuwasawa Design School in Tokyo when I was a teenager. While there, I heard about designer Shiro Kuramata. His works gave me a new perspective on furniture design; they enlightened me. I wanted to become a creator with an attitude similar to Kuramata's. I was fortunate enough to work under him for a year. Then I was introduced to Issey Miyake, and I started working for him. Mr Miyake is also an unconventional designer. He encouraged me to explore new ways of making and allowed me to design the scenography and installation for his exhibition. But the design was for the Issey Miyake brand, so I thought: *what if Issey Mikaye were designing this?* It was about *his* identity, not my own self-expression.'

'My career changed course in 2000, when I established my own office. I had been nurturing some of my own ideas while working at Issey Miyake. My first project was the office itself, which I built from scratch rather than renting a furnished space. I brought in wooden beams and poles from a 150-year-old demolished rice granary in Shimane Prefecture in western Japan. I combined them with industrial materials, and at the time it was quite rare to mix old natural materials with modern industrial ones. The use of both was a statement to myself – the statement of a man looking towards the future while also being aware of the history of design. My work is firmly rooted in what I've learned from the past.'

'Honey-Pop, a chair I designed in 2000, represented a ground-breaking moment in my career. Realized in 2001, it was an exploration in making a chair with a honeycomb structure. Layers of two-dimensional paper unfold to form a three-dimensional object. I wanted to find out how to make a chair in a brand-new way. It was my challenge to the chair and its history. I initially presented it at Milan Design Week, and it kick-started my career.'

'My work falls into two categories. One is for the industry and involves a client; in that case, my objective is to meet the client's needs. The second is personally initiated work; no one asks me to make it. I have stacks of drawings and sketches of ideas long in the making. They don't necessarily have to be realized.'

'I always try to create something that doesn't yet exist. The idea for Pane came about when I was considering how to make a chair without a conventional frame of wire or wood. Ultimately, I used bundles of thin polyester fibres to form the structure and to distribute the user's weight, while also offering comfort to the sitter. The chair was realized in 2006, but it took three years to develop.'

'I look into many methods for realizing my products. The larger my stock of methods, the better chance I have of making what I've designed. My past experiments can be modified and applied to different projects.'

'*Why am I doing this? I'm not doing any productive work*: a thought that sometimes comes into my head when I'm deadlocked. I feel hopeless.'

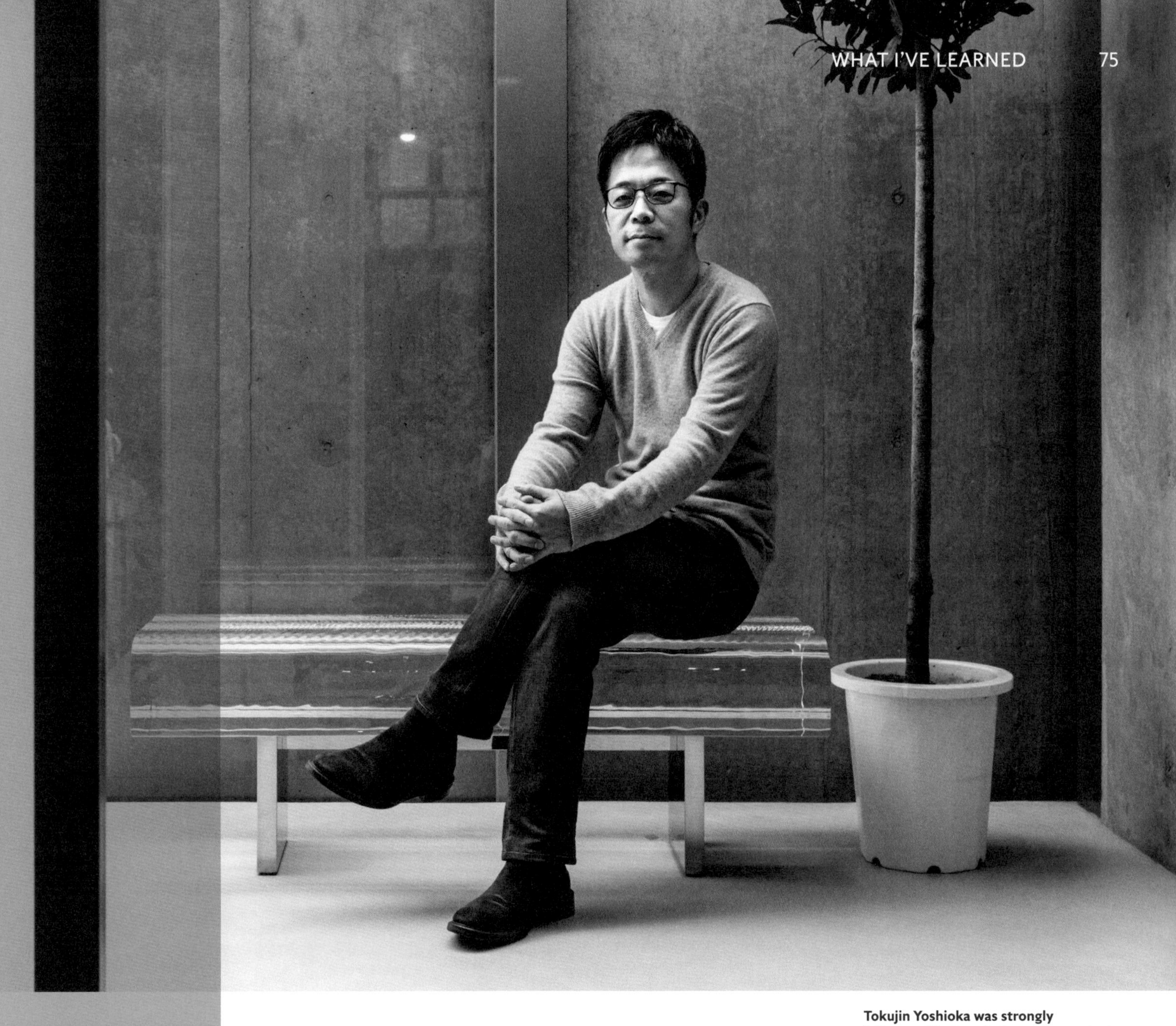

Tokujin Yoshioka was strongly influenced by two designers he worked with: Shiro Kuramata and Issey Miyake.

'I research the past and envision the future. But to realize my vision, I need craftspeople, engineers, manufacturers – the hands and skills of many. Because my designs are unprecedented, people don't know how to realize what they're looking at – they tell me what I'm trying to do is impossible. Earlier on in my career, people didn't want to go out on a limb for a young designer with no credentials. I couldn't direct them to do what I wanted, so I started by using my own hands. In a way, being told something is impossible can be the shortest way to get a project going. Gradually, people began to understand my passion and my ideas; they challenged themselves to overcome the obstacles and make it work.'

'My career as an independent designer spans more than 20 years. During that time, I've come to the conclusion that compromise doesn't help my work to be actualized. A trade-off may be important at some stage if you want your designs to be produced commercially. But for my personal work, no. Because there are already enough objects in the world, I always think about the significance of bringing out a new product – about whether what I'm making is really a milestone. Pursuing a project is the consequence of long reflection about its implications. I need to be insistent, almost obstinate, to achieve my intention, because a trade-off is a trade-off. Compromise results in a different outcome.'

'I don't necessarily intend to make new forms; I intend to evoke emotions, to touch people's senses and make them joyful. I like to think that design is a good way to do this.'

'As I designer, I'm not content to wait for clients to come to me – or even for someone to say that I can make whatever I want if it's also something for them. I don't want to face the ifs, ands or buts that go with the inability to realize an idea just because I wasn't commissioned to do it. I will do it myself if I think the idea is significant. That's why I proposed a plan – which includes stadium, logo and torch – for the 2020 Olympic Games in Tokyo. I'm not an architect, so my concept won't be selected for the design of a new national stadium. But the Olympics aren't just a sporting event; they will change the social system. I simply wanted to present my idea for such an epic event.'

'In the end, I guess that more than mesmerizing *others*, I want to see the unseen *myself*.'

tokujin.com

Tables

Dutch architect Ronald Hooft brings his *ideas to the table.*

Portrait and styling **Anne Claire de Breij**

The table is more than simply the prime test facing every self-respecting product designer – and, believe me, the numbers are staggering. The design of the table is also – and I say this without hesitation, despite the lack of a scientifically supported study to back me up – an indication of social movements.

In the 1950s, table design was characterized by society's scramble to leave the war years behind. An air of optimism emerged in the form of lightweight, brightly coloured Formica tabletops resting on slender legs. Many of these designs – with their aerodynamic, kidney-shaped tops and fragile fundaments – looked like objects poised to fly away.

You might say the post-war era came to an end when Saarinen presented his iconic design to Knoll. Saarinen's cast-aluminium base, seemingly dripping from the underside of the table to form a pool of liquid on the floor, was a harbinger of the space age – of the future as pictured throughout the world at that time, with hover-mobiles and robots ready to step in and take over the more onerous household tasks.

A need for transparency marked the post-hippie era. It could hardly have been accidental that glass tabletops began springing up like mushrooms here, there and everywhere. Thick sheets of green glass were coupled with bases made from wood, marble, various noble metals, stainless steel and brass. At the beginning of the materialistic 1980s, the most decadent of such pieces featured in television series like *Dallas* and *Dynasty*. It's impossible to erase the image of a silk-gowned Joan Collins, lavish fur stole caressing her shoulders, sipping pink champagne at a glass-topped breakfast table that drew the eyes down to the tusks of a pair of African elephants, which added to the opulence.

Around the dawn of the new millennium, tables grew more and more robust. Designers translated the desire for sustainability and security into tables with heavy solid-wood tops and, in many cases, angular legs made from the same material. Although the legions of enormous trees required for their manufacture is incompatible with the sustainability concept, these tables are virtually indestructible, which speaks in their behalf.

Visitors to the January edition of the Cologne furniture fair, with its vast presentation of latest-generation dining tables, saw a great many paper-thin tops. Long. Gravity-defying. Unbelievable spans. Precious materials. Lovely tropical timbers and exotic types of marble in an array of colours.

A really good look at everything on display at the fair also revealed more than a few kidney-shaped tops on svelte legs; curvaceous stems resembling fluid drops elegantly crafted from solid timber; glass tops in every size and shape; bases in brass, bronze and stainless steel; and weighty examples with tops of unfinished wood, suggesting the need for a serious hoist to lift them into the house.

What do these designs have to say about the zeitgeist? I haven't the faintest idea. What I do know is that anybody who's looking for a new dining table this year has a multitude of choices. ●

CLOTHING Sunglasses by Vava Eyewear and jacket by The Suits (both courtesy of Sprmrkt); model's own T-shirt; jeans by Boris Bidjan Saberi, courtesy of ZPK; socks by Bjorn Borg OBJECTS Tray Table by Hay and uncredited tube vase (both courtesy of The Frozen Fountain)

She + Me = Us

Nipa Doshi and Jonathan Levien orchestrate family, work and music to achieve a *rhythmically balanced life.*

Words **Floor Kuitert**
Portrait **Winter Vandenbrink**

She adapts her song repertoire to his morning yoga sessions, and his physical approach to work complements her sketches: Nipa Doshi and Jonathan Levien could hardly be more compatible.

j

JONATHAN LEVIEN: My day starts earlier than it used to. Combining work and family leaves very few hours in the day to do something for myself. So I get up at 5:30 and wander around a bit before beginning an hour of ashtanga yoga. It gets my mind in the right place, sets me up for the day. Nipa starts her day with singing. She's studying Indian classical singing, and the morning is almost the only time she has to practise. Nipa often sings something suitable for a morning yoga session. We're very compatible.

Music is more than a hobby – it's very much part of our life. So is theatre. We go to the opera and are intimately involved in the world of performance. In my opinion, there is absolutely a connection between music, rhythm and design. You can compare musical rhythm to visual rhythm. People who learn to play an instrument or who engage in other cultural activities develop an interesting sensibility. In our case, it feeds into our work, even though we're not consciously trying to make that happen.

We live in the Barbican, which is at the heart of the City of London. Our studio is in Shoreditch, on Columbia Road, in an old furniture factory that's about a ten-minute bicycle ride from our home. On Sundays, Columbia Road is an amazing place to buy flowers. The factory is flanked on either side by a school and a park. We have the pleasant sound of children playing during the day, and we also have some green. The studio is a big open space filled with natural light; it has wooden floors and a very industrial feel. Quite a contrast to where we live. The Barbican is a sort of utopian concrete building. But there are also connections between work and home, because a lot of the things we have in our home are prototypes of things we've made. What I love is the contrast between the highly designed, highly architectural Barbican and the rather uncoordinated arrangement of the objects we surround ourselves with at home. Those pieces came into our home over the years and simply found places for themselves.

Nipa never works at home. The act of going to work and sitting down at a desk is vital to her creativity. I sketch quite a bit at home, but for me work is a very physical thing. I make. I sculpt. I shape pieces in three dimensions. Those things have to be done in the studio.

We've had a scooter for 15 years now. That's how we get around. Nipa hates the look of the thing, but she's a faithful pillion rider. It's a superb way to get around in London. We beat all the other traffic.

Most mornings at the studio we manage ongoing projects and brief the team. We also spend time with our staff developing new projects.

We are very fortunate to have a nice restaurant on the ground floor of our building. Brawn serves tapas-style food – very tempting around lunchtime. Sometimes we go home for a lunch prepared by our cook. We don't like to eat out every day. Even when we go home, we're back in the studio quickly. The period after lunch is usually intensively creative. It's a time for drawing and for really getting into a project. Afternoons are for working together with Nipa. Those moments are precious. It's when things really happen for us.

We finish work around 6:30. Leaving the studio is always a rush, and often as we're closing up shop, we feel obligated to stay and finish one or more 'urgent' matters. It's not easy to get Nipa out the door.

Switching off after work is not something we do. It's something that happens to us. Home life takes over. We have a seven-year-old son, who's fantastic. He demands our attention from the moment he sees us in the evening until the moment he goes to sleep. Having a child means separating your work life from your home life. There's no other way.

Our daily routine disappears when we're travelling. It's difficult to get back into the normal swing of things when we get home. I have to make a conscious effort to do so.

I play the tabla, a pair of Indian drums. I like to practise in the evenings for an hour or so. And I do taekwondo twice a week, from 7:00 to 8:00 p.m. I have plenty of time to pursue my interests, but to do that, you need to be able to *focus*. ●

At the Salone del Mobile, Doshi Levien continues its campaign for Bolon (see page 134), while also presenting new collections for Hay, B&B Italia, Moroso and Kettal
doshilevien.com

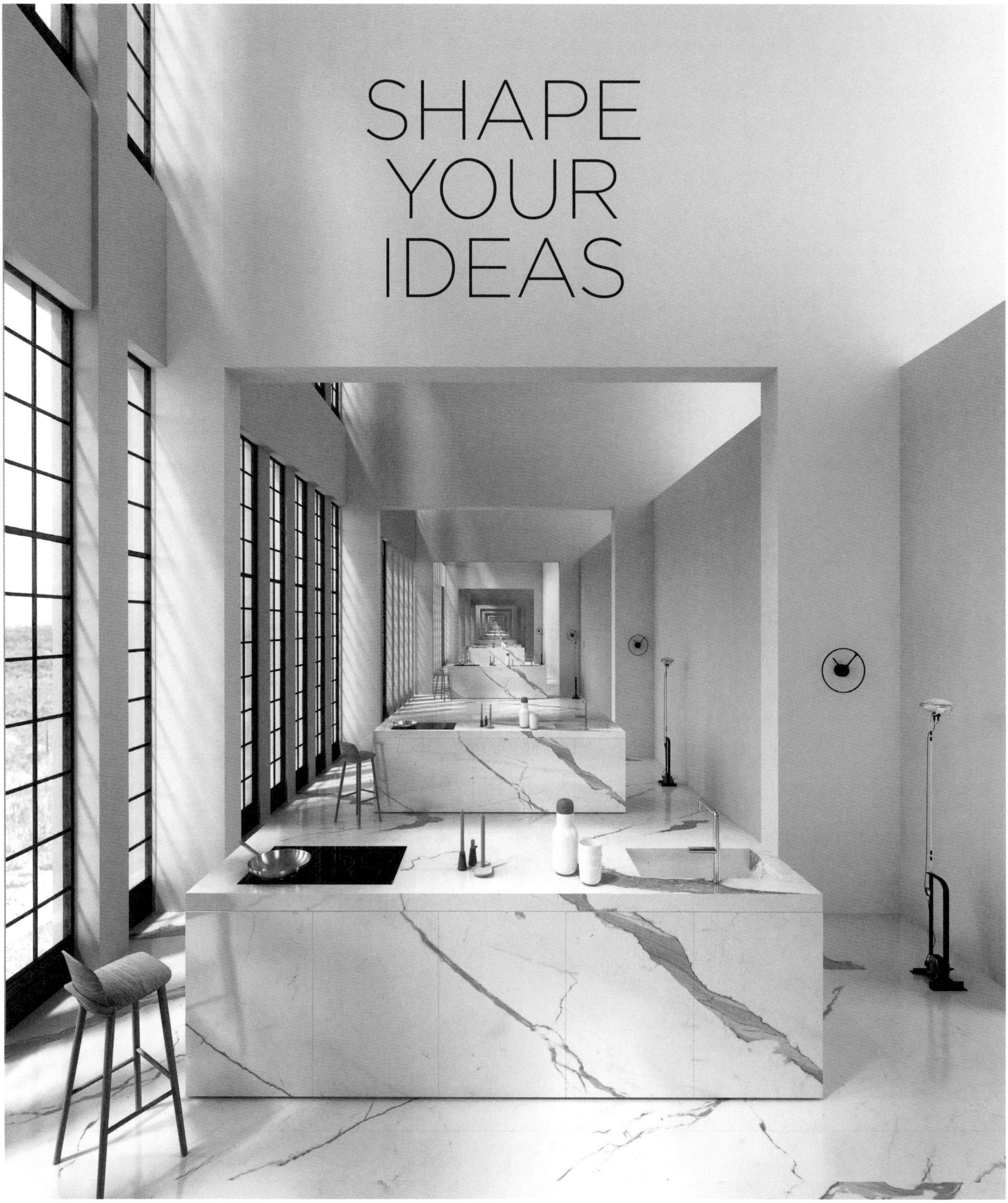

Within Reach

Marieke Sanders and her husband don't treat their design collection as untouchable art. ***Each and every item is put to use.***

Words **Anne van der Zwaag** Photos **Cindy Baar**

Photographic works by the likes of Viviane Sassen are bold additions to the Sanders' home. The table and chair are by Jasper Morrison.

Collectors Pieter and Marieke Sanders live in a monumental house next to Teylers Museum, in the historical centre of Haarlem. Like other members of the Sanders family, for years they have been welcome guests at art fairs and galleries. Theirs is an art-loving community, and they play an active role in the Dutch art world. I met Marieke in her function as president of the Wertheimer Stichting, a not-for-profit foundation that promotes Dutch photography. She is also one of the founders of Art Table, a club for women with an interest in art. The couple regularly open their home to fellow collectors in the Netherlands and from abroad.

Today we're relaxing in their living room, which is filled with art and design objects. They see a significant difference between the two. Art is collected based on its autonomous value, while they view design as an applied discipline. Pieter admits that art sometimes evokes associations with design, and vice versa. As an example, he points to an abstract refrigerator in the corner of the room, made by artist Jan van Munster. Marieke's explanation takes the idea a step further: 'You can sit on this bench by Joep van Lieshout or lay something on it, but the object is intended as a work of art.

'We like to collect design objects that are functional,' she says. 'Look at the door handles in our home, all designed by Jasper Morrison. We've replaced the original hinges and locks on all the doors and cabinets with different designs from his series, giving the old doors a unique character.' Pieter says that 'design has to be serviceable and fit into a given environment. In our house, that environment is aimed first and foremost at the display of contemporary art, which changes on a regular basis. We like to see our new acquisitions right away; the rest – say 60 to 70 per cent – remain in storage.' That's a shame, according to the collectors, and that is why they regularly loan works to museums and art institutions.

You can be a successful collector without making huge investments

A chandelier designed by Richard Hutten for the Centraal Museum Utrecht ended the Sanders' search for a lamp that worked with an existing decorative ceiling element.

On two occasions, they have donated a substantial number of works: once to the Stedelijk Museum in Amsterdam and once to the Cultural Heritage Agency of the Netherlands, in total about 20 per cent of their collection at the time. The donation to the Stedelijk – around 120 pieces – was a gift in honour of the museum's reopening. When asked whether they would ever sell anything, their reaction is resolute: 'Never! We donate because work that enters the public domain allows more people to get pleasure from it.'

Pieter and Marieke Sanders are emphatically not investors; they buy art in order to enjoy it. Marieke continues: 'You can be a successful collector without making huge investments. If we went to major galleries to buy famous names, the prices would be quickly out of reach for us.' The trick is to discover talent and buy early. 'Art and design are seen increasingly as investments, but in the Netherlands there are few collectors who can buy on an unlimited budget,' she says. 'We have always focused on young emerging artists with new concepts and ideas. Some are world famous now, like Marijke van Warmerdam. In the beginning, we collected mainly paintings and objects; photography and video work came later.'

They have been collecting for about 40 years. 'First we dressed our house with pieces borrowed from the family, which we gradually replaced with objects we bought ourselves. This original Miller chair was one of our first furniture purchases in the 1960s. The design was very new and far above our budget, but we wanted it. So we lived a few days on bread and water.' She laughs. 'We bought all the vintage pieces at the time they were designed. In terms of design, our interior is a mix of family heirlooms, like this 17th-century cabinet, mid-century design and contemporary pieces, such as the table by Maarten Baas and the lamp by Richard Hutten.

'We searched a long time for a beautiful ceiling lamp to hang above the table. A large antique decorative element on the ceiling makes it difficult to hang just anything. And because we want to be able to move the table, we need a lamp that doesn't hang too low. »

We discovered the Hutten lamp at the Centraal Museum Utrecht, along with a large collection of Dutch design. It fits here perfectly.'

'In addition to this house and our country house in Drenthe, where we also have land art on display, we have a gallery space here in Haarlem,' says Pieter. 'We show other things there,' says Marieke. 'One example is video work.' She's not keen on the term 'gallery space' and suggests 'art space', a designation used by Americans. All their collections can be visited only by appointment. Keeping track of the art demands a lot of work, most of which they do themselves. 'It's all very personal,' says Pieter. 'We don't aspire to run our own museum; the existence of our "warehouse" – or "art space" – is already an enormous luxury.'

Although they rarely commission pieces, a series of three bookcases occupying a prominent place in the dining room was created specifically for Pieter and Marieke by German designer Nils Holger Moormann. 'They're normally available only in white and black, but because we bought so many, he made them in red for us. It's just a matter of asking, even though it might cost a bit more. We find that designers are open to people who think along with them.' Marieke reminds him that artists don't react the same way.

'Designers often like the idea of adapting their work to suit a certain setting,' says Pieter. 'We've also thought about an assignment for Marcel Wanders or Studio Job, but they mainly do large projects, and then the homey feeling quickly gets lost. Art and life are our priorities, and both need space to be and to continue to be. We want to be able to make changes easily, and the interior should not compete with the works.'

All their design pieces are being used. Not one is exhibited – or purchased – as art. 'We bought this rug by Wanders three years ago, simply because of how well it suits our interior. Heleen de Ruijter, former owner of Galerie Binnen, was our interior-design consultant, but in principle we always do everything as a couple, including purchases. Many collectors start with an adviser and gradually take over, but we've done it our way – very intuitively – from the beginning,' says Marieke. Pieter mentions the need to develop an eye for quality, but he realizes that might be easy for them to say: 'A background like ours makes us familiar with the phenomenon; we feel at home in this element.

The interior should not compete with the works

'We usually buy art and design through a gallery or shop, rarely from the artists or designers themselves,' he says. 'In the past, you had fewer galleries than now, which perhaps made it easier. We looked at about ten in Amsterdam, and started with Dutch artists. We also bought work by foreign artists in Dutch galleries, and in the past ten years the collection has become truly international. There's an incredible amount available; you have to find your own way and look into whatever appeals to you. We follow artists and designers, but we collect in breadth, not depth.

'We don't work with specific galleries, but among those we visit regularly are three in Amsterdam: Ron Mandos, Annet Gelink and Van Zomeren. They are very active internationally and are key intermediaries. But things change. Sometimes you have temporary preferences, or a gallery starts to follow a different course. This is exactly why fairs like Basel, Madrid, Miami and Rotterdam are so important; everyone's there and you have a nice overview of the current range, all in one place.

'We heartily recommend collecting; it enriches your life. That's why we included our children in our enthusiasm for art and design. Our daughter now owns a small photography collection, and our son set up Nieuw Dakota, runs the Livingstone Gallery in The Hague and is building an eclectic collection of his own. When they reached adulthood, they followed in our footsteps by decorating their homes with pieces from our collection, which they are beginning to exchange for personal purchases.' Pieter animatedly recalls giving the children a few thousand guilders – quite some time ago – to spend at Art Amsterdam. The money they didn't spend had to be returned to their parents. Good motivation, because: you can't start early enough. ●

sanderscollection.nl

The Sanders' interior combines family heirlooms and mid-century design with such contemporary pieces as the Clay table by Maarten Baas and door handles by Jasper Morrison.

Red Thread

Favouring just two colours of yarn, Chiharu Shiota *weaves infinite stories* in her site-specific installations.

Words **Anna Sansom** Portrait **Daniel Hofer**

Born in Japan, Chiharu Shiota studied painting in Tokyo before being educated under Marina Abramovic at the Braunschweig University of Art in Germany and completing her schooling at the University of the Arts in Berlin, the city in which she now resides. A desire to draw in the air led her to use yarn – usually black and red – in her work. She makes large-scale, site-specific installations that involve threads woven from floor to ceiling, enmeshing everyday objects such as beds, dresses, musical instruments and keys. After representing Japan at the Venice Biennale in 2015 (*Frame* 106, p. 130), Shiota presented a solo show, Sleeping Is Like Death, at Galerie Daniel Templon in Brussels earlier this year. During a performance at the opening, three young women appeared to be asleep in hospital beds.

How did you become interested in using yarn in your work? CHIHARU SHIOTA: When I was a student, I was in the painting department and I wanted to a draw – but in three dimensions, not two. So I started making lines with string in the air – in space – when I was about 20.

You use black or red string in your installations. What do these colours signify for you? Black is the universe. It's like the night sky – deep and dark. Red is something inside, like the body or blood. Red is what's inside me, and black is what's outside. The two come together in my work.

How would you describe the process of making an installation? I have 70 per cent of what I do in my head before I start weaving, but the final result always turns out to be different from what I'd envisioned. I rely on my imagination and try not to make drawings first, because when I draw something, I feel that the work is already finished. I like to bring materials to the site and start making something there. Things made in the studio beforehand are less dynamic, and often they don't fit into the space. My work is more about drawing in the space by weaving than about responding to architecture. My eyes are still those of a painter. »

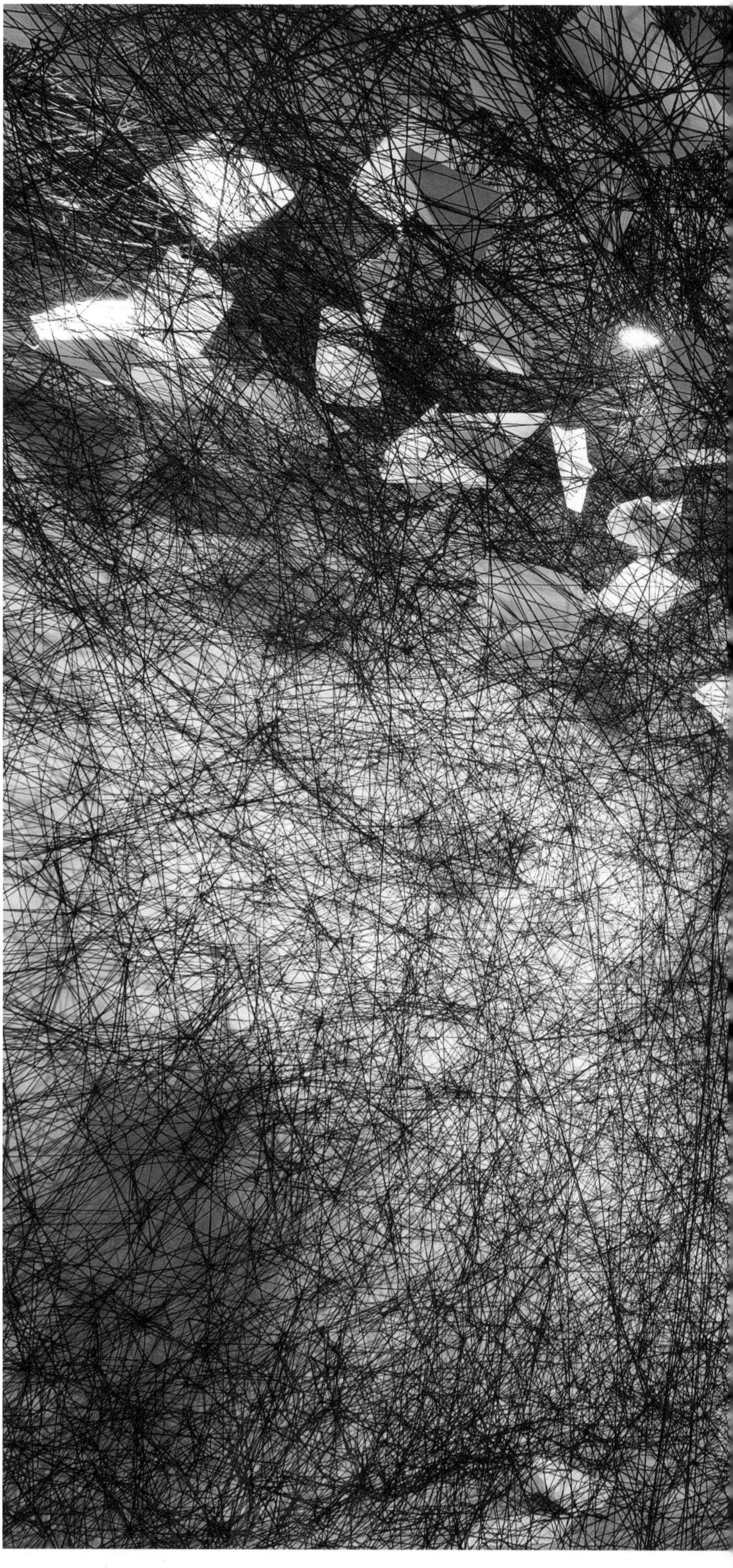

Photo Sunhi Mang, courtesy of Chiharu Shiota

A Long Day, **Shiota's solo show at K21 in Düsseldorf, features an old desk, an old chair and sheets of paper trapped like insects in a billowing web of black threads.**

Photo Isabelle Arthuis, courtesy of Chiharu Shiota and Galerie Daniel Templon

***Sleeping Is Like Death*, an exhibition at Galerie Daniel Templon in Brussels, incorporated beds, an important theme in Shiota's art. For her, beds signify the 'beginning and the end of life'.**

"My work is more about weaving in the space than about responding to architecture

You first made an installation with beds in 2000. What led you to revisit the idea in a more open, dynamic style for your exhibition at Galerie Daniel Templon in Brussels? The bed is important to me. Many people are born and die in a bed, making the bed the beginning and the end of life – and a place filled with stories. I wanted to make an installation with beds, but in a new style. When I sleep, I sometimes feel that I can't wake up any more. And when I do wake up, even though my brain is working, I'm still dreaming. It's this kind of world that I wanted to create, within a space that would show dreaming, reality and movement. At the gallery in Brussels, people could walk into and through the installation, whereas the piece I made in 2000 kept them outside, where they could only walk around it.

How does this installation differ from *The Key in the Hand* at the Venice Biennale? There it was about weaving from the ceiling downwards. The threads carried the weight of the keys, a combined load of one tonne. In Brussels I was able to extend the woven threads across the dimensions of the space. The work was freer, like a wave, and had much more feeling, so that dreams could envelop the sleepers.

How do you choose which objects to use? I pick ordinary things that human beings use every day, like a key or a suitcase. I travel a lot, so I often use a suitcase. Seeing either of these objects conjures up memories and stories, which inspire me to start weaving.

How do people respond to your work? I would say that people generally feel they *belong* to my art pieces, as they often talk about how engaging my installations can be. My goal is to express human emotions through my objects, and people tend to find my work touching.

What are you going to show at the Sydney Biennale? *Conscious Sleep* will be on Cockatoo Island [near Sydney Harbour]. The site was formerly a prison, so the work will be about convicts sleeping. The prison's inmates didn't have beds; they slept on the floor. I'm using 20 beds, propped up diagonally against the walls. It's a metaphor for my thoughts about more than 100 prisoners sleeping together in a small room. ●

Chiharu Shiota is participating in the Biennale of Sydney (until 5 June 2016) and is also showing work that occupies one of the Artist's Rooms at K21 in Düsseldorf until July 2016
chiharu-shiota.com

The **Human**ist

When it comes to designing for the workplace, Koleksiyon's Koray Malhan stresses the *importance of the individual*.

Words **Shonquis Moreno** Portraits **Çağlar Kanzik**

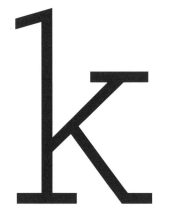

Koleksiyon design and brand director Koray Malhan was born in 1972, the same year that his father, Turkish architect Faruk Malhan, launched the Istanbul-based furniture brand. Today the company has 23 showrooms in locations worldwide, from Dallas to Darmstadt, Lima to Baku. The latest addition opened in Manhattan last June. In conjunction with running the business, Malhan *fils* plays an important part as one of its designers. In this role, Malhan parses his complex philosophical meditations into graphically minimalist furnishings. And it's no wonder: when he was a child, Malhan's parents – his mother is a sociologist – had him poring over the likes of Friedrich Engels and Sigmund Freud. In conversations about design, he quotes Pier Paolo Pasolini, Jean-Luc Godard, James Joyce and Umberto Eco. Having recently resumed the study of classical piano, he talks about tonality and the subdominant septet, Arnold Schönberg and musicologist Theodor Adorno. With degrees in industrial design and furniture design from Istanbul's Mimar Sinan Fine Arts University and London's Ravensbourne College of Design and Communication, Malhan applies the structural abstractions of music, literature and art to design and architecture to create 'open work' products. Rather than restricting the brand's output to broad, single solutions for all, Malhan designs products that serve as the building blocks from which designers and users can create site- and human-specific 'topographies'.

'I couldn't imagine a life without design,' says Malhan. His earliest memories are of his parents building the business at their dining-room table, which was cluttered with projects and plans in a house filled with friends who themselves traded in creativity, as playwrights, actors, novelists or musicians. He would often visit his father's workshop in Ankara and, after the age of 13, spent his summers working there. His mother's influence ensures that Malhan's design practice begins with the human, in general, and individual human beings, specifically.

Designed by Malhan *père*, Koleksiyon's offices say a great deal about the firm's views on design for the workplace. Its Istanbul headquarters, situated on an unusually verdant campus in a city hungry for green space, consist of an elegant cluster of buildings containing showrooms, multidisciplinary classrooms, a well-stocked library and a café. 'Design for the office is less about design than it is about people,' Malhan says. 'When we talk about collaborative workspaces, we're not talking about trends, but about people from different disciplines acting in more collaborative ways. The idea is to replace *me* spaces with *us* spaces.' In a country where many offices are still bound by a rigid pecking order, more than 75 per cent of Koleksiyon's customers are

“ Design for the office is less about design

Koleksiyon

ESTABLISHED 1972
HEADQUARTERS Istanbul, London, New York City
EMPLOYEES 750
BESTSELLING PRODUCTS Partita, Borges and Barbari desk systems; Gala and Halia office chairs; Song storage system; Ikaros and Dilim sofas; Suri pouf
PRODUCT RANGE Desk systems, office chairs, storage systems, sofas, armchairs, coffee tables, partition wall systems
CORE MARKETS USA, UK, Turkey, Central Europe, UAE
PRODUCTION SITE 86,000 m^2
SHOWROOMS 23 worldwide

global, entrepreneurial, democratically organized businesses. As a result, Malhan envisions a future with a greater emphasis on collaboration and designs 'against hierarchy'.

In 2010 the brand's approach to 'co-creative environments' took the form of desks, cabinets, sofas, tables and storage units, each a part of larger work 'habitats' that can be combined to form 'neighbourhoods'. 'We are interested in treating work areas like cities,' he says, 'dedicating space and furniture to communal use.' In 2008 Malhan designed Ikaros, a workstation-sofa that doubles as collaborative space and a 'refuge' from the distractions of the over-connected desk. In collaboration with Italy's Studio Kairos, Koleksiyon created Borges in 2014 to 'destroy the standard workstation' by making the work surface dramatically shelflike. Around this shelf-axis an ecology grows, supported by small tablets for temporary work, meeting and split tables for collaboration, and personal hoods for performing concentrated tasks in a limited amount of time. The idea, he explains, 'is to present all these elements freely, so that no assembly is needed. Every item can be easily moved or removed by the user throughout the course of the day without the use of tools.' He calls it 'a self-made topography'.

Malhan's Oblivion series comprises pods – shaped like cones and inverted cones – that disrupt the open-plan environment with sheltering moments by establishing 'landmarks' in the office for collective use. Vertical posts and brackets support horizontal surfaces to form tables, shelves and cantilevered seating. An Oblivion pod – microarchitecture for the workplace – can serve as library, research capsule, study space, coffee hub or presentation room. Shared by colleagues but belonging to none, it cultivates communal habits without losing sight of the individual.

For a man who spent his childhood watching the living room morph daily from drafting to dinner table and back again, this approach to design is natural. As if to echo the past, many of Koleksiyon's products use tactile woods and lush fabrics to cover unexpected surfaces. Koleksiyon furniture places not just the user at the centre of its design, but a diversity of human beings, and that is Malhan's vision of where the future is heading – towards touch as much as tech, interpretation rather than repetition, openness instead of closure. ●

koleksiyoninternational.com

A desk-cum-sofa, Koray Malhan's Ikaros (left) is intended for both individual and communal use. Roomy armrests and a flat extension of the backrest double as easy-to-use work surfaces.

Stroke of **Luk**

Christina Luk hopes the recognition gained from Lukstudio's small-scale interiors will allow her to *tackle more serious issues*.

Words **Michael Webb** Portraits **Olivier H. Dressen**

'There's a noodle-soup outlet on every corner in China, so the client wanted the design of Noodle Rack to create a name for his product,' says Luk, who included draped wires in the interior, a reference to the restaurant's staple offering.

You grew up in Hong Kong, studied art and architecture in London and Toronto, and then relocated to Shanghai, where you established your own studio. Why did you decide to make design your career? CHRISTINA LUK: I've always loved the concept of beauty. Like most kids, I drew and doodled. My mum thought I could put that talent to use and encouraged me to take drawing classes. I realized that was the path I wanted to follow and can't think of anything else I would rather be doing. I was quite good at math when I was young, but I knew I didn't want to deal with numbers – even though sometimes I have to. Working in design gives you the opportunity to solve problems and to create. Now that I have my own team, passing on knowledge to them and seeing them grow is really gratifying.

What have you learned from living on three continents? The biggest transition was leaving home for London, where I studied for three years, before spending another ten years in Toronto. The pace is different in the West. All Hong Kongers have a passion for speed and effective solutions. Even in the arts, you try to arrive at a result right away. In London it took me a while to embrace a different world of process and experimentation – of time used to explore the unknowns. Going to art and architecture schools abroad encouraged me to take it easy and be open-minded, and I liked the ethnic diversity of Toronto. Now I've been away from Hong Kong for as long as I lived there, but I still feel that I need to identify goals and achieve them.

Why did you choose to settle in Shanghai? I found it very exciting when I first came to work here, with lots of opportunities to design. Shanghai is not China; it's an international hub – the New York of the Orient – a place that the Chinese look to for new ideas. It's a platform for the best talent, with a constant influx of interesting speakers and exhibitions. And it has a culture of the custom-made. When we meet, the talk is about where to get clothes or furniture made. People are very receptive to innovative ideas or a reinterpretation of traditions. I don't pretend to know the city that well, though; my life revolves around my home, office and yoga studio.

What does your office space say about your firm? It's homey, and our multicultural team is a bit like a family. I've never understood designers who spend a lot of time getting everything right for their clients while neglecting their own work environment. Toronto gave me a love of nature, so I was excited about adapting a house that opens onto a tree-shaded courtyard and is full of natural light. Working so closely together has made us good communicators. One of my helpers comes in to cook lunch for us twice a week, so we get to socialize. We also take ten-minute breaks outside. Six to eight people work for Lukstudio at present, and we probably won't grow much larger. I'll be 39 this year, and the others are all younger. Each has strengths and weaknesses, but because we're a start-up, they have to be multitalented in order to tackle every aspect of a job. »

The team at Lukstudio (left to right): Christina Luk, PaoYee Lim, Ray Ou, Marcello Chiadò Rana, Yiye Lin, Cai Jin Hong and Leo Wang. Alba Beroiz Blazquez is absent.

“Clients demand that everything be fast, economical and have a wow factor

The Chinese look to Shanghai for new ideas

For Aimé Patisserie, Lukstudio translated the brand's packaging – a box with four semicircular leaves of rice paper – into the wall and ceiling of its interior design.

Photos Peter Dixie

What are your guiding design principles? We try to create something with a strong identity that serves the client's needs. We reinterpret everyday objects in our work, assembling them in an artistic way to give them new life. Surprise is another important ingredient. We try to engage our users and make them remember us as the makers of the space. Each project is a unique journey, having to do with the chemistry of the people involved. It's important for us to explore different forms and find new concepts; I don't want to churn out more of the same. Once we've proven ourselves as creative people, we'll be able to explore more serious issues, such as sustainable architecture and the design of innovative products.

What would you like to be doing five years from now? We're currently working on retail and restaurants, and we'd like to diversify. Cultural and institutional projects. Schools and public housing. We approach all our projects as architecture, thinking more about space than finishes, and we'd like to be able to design those spaces from the ground up.

How do you rate the Chinese design community in comparison with their peers worldwide? If you are a talented designer, China is the place to be. There's a strong demand for spatial design: often the buildings here work as objects but are badly planned and executed inside. Despite the downturn in the economy, people are still flooding into Shanghai. But it's not easy. We have to communicate and work harder to meet very tight schedules. Clients demand that everything be fast, economical and have a wow factor. On the plus side, you don't have a long wait for permits. We've started to collaborate with a few contractors, but they have to be quite brave to work with us. To make sure something happens, you have to push. That's exciting, and because we're young we still have fire inside us. ●

lukstudiodesign.com

'16
DESIGN
DISTRICT
THE BEST TRADE EVENT FOR INTERIOR DESIGN
June 1-2-3 2016
TAETS-ZAANDAM
WWW.DESIGNDISTRICT.NL

Noteworthy

Swedish design studio Note pinpoints *five significant projects* in its diverse portfolio.

Words **Daniel Golling** Portrait **Mikael Olsson**

Marginal Notes was a huge risk that paid off. Note invested all its time and energy in creating objects of self-expression, some of which later went into production.

2011
Marginal Notes *exhibition*

'It changed our world.' Cristiano Pigazzini, design manager at Note, is talking about Marginal Notes, an exhibition his company presented at Stockholm Design Week 2011. His words explain *what* Marginal Notes did for Note, which comprised nine members at the time. But in order to understand *why* the studio not only challenged the current taste and discourse of contemporary Swedish and Scandinavian design, but also risked everything to do so – roughly €100,000 – it might be best to paint a picture of the situation five years ago.

Whatever a 'conventional design studio' might be, that's what Pigazzini and his colleagues claim that Note was at the time: a team of eight designers, with specialities ranging from graphics to interiors. And let's not forget Pigazzini himself, whose skills are more in the management field. There was talent abound, but Note felt trapped working in such an established way. 'We did well financially,' says Pigazzini, 'but not psychologically. We didn't have an expression of our own, and we felt that we were able to do so much more.' Pigazzini and his staff wanted to prove themselves. The feeling was so strong that in September 2010 they put everything else aside and devoted all their time and money to what would become Marginal Notes.

The exhibition took place in a furniture showroom in central Stockholm. The room was crammed with roughly 15 products, including lamps, stools, sofas and cabinets, as well as seemingly functionless objects. United by the lavish use of colour and a collage aesthetic, the pieces suggested – particularly in retrospect – the path that Note would pave for Swedish design and, at the same time, highlighted what happens when designers are free to create without restrictions.

The risk was worth the effort. The show brought Note a great deal of attention and appreciation, while giving the studio a blueprint for the future. The designers learned what they were capable of and how to organize their work. 'To us, Marginal Notes marked a transition – like before and after, or BC and AD.'

It's comical to think that something not intended for production became an award-winning stool

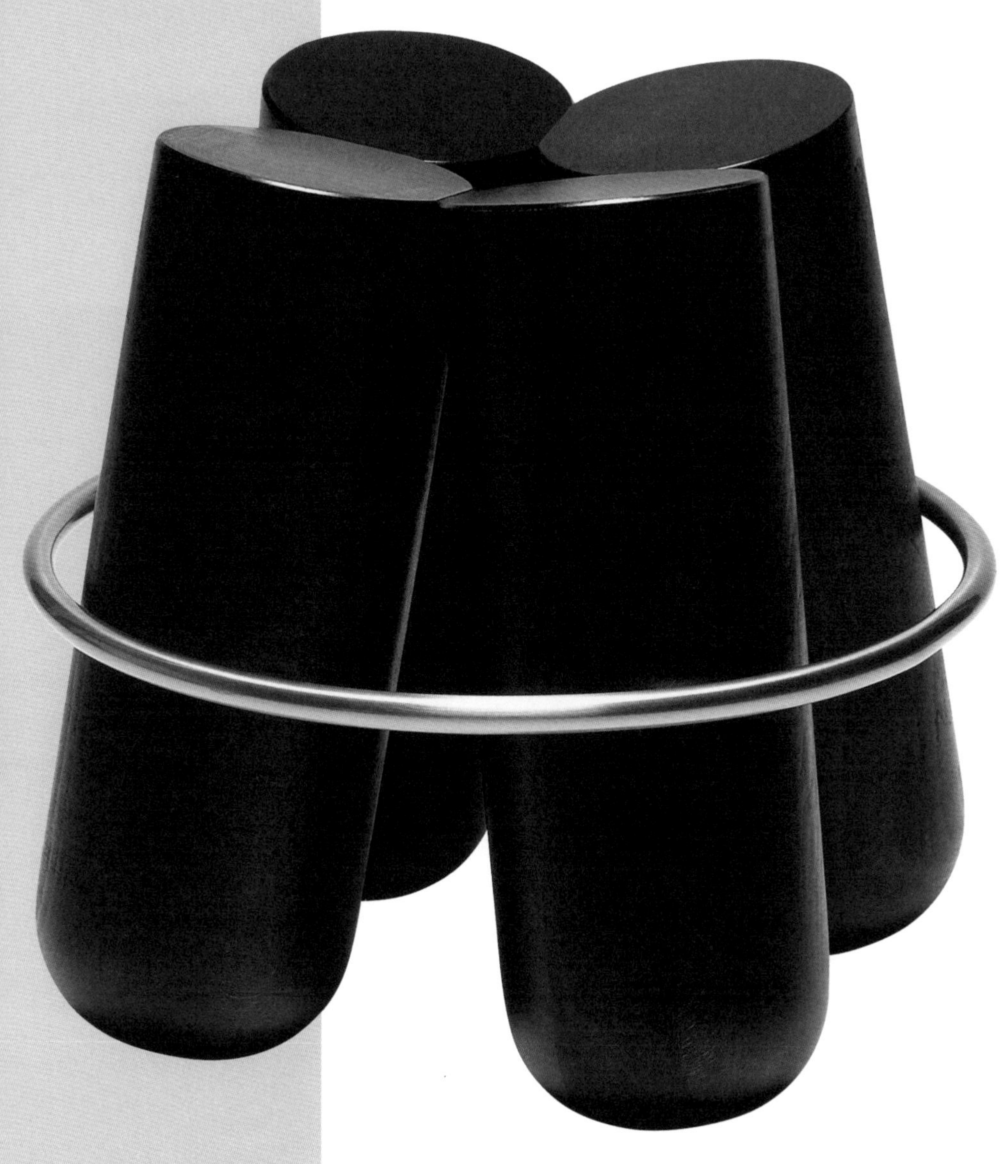

French brand La Chance's first collection included Bolt, a stool Note originally designed for its Marginal Notes exhibition. Adopting a new nonhierarchical way of working, Note's creatives submitted sketches and voted on the final design.

2012
Bolt *stool*

'We never imagined that any of the Marginal Notes pieces would be put into production,' says Pigazzini. An e-mail from La Chance was the catalyst to a process that proved them wrong. The French brand was launched during the 2012 Salone del Mobile as part of Tom Dixon's Most, a platform for creative innovation at the National Museum of Science and Technology in Milan. Two pieces from Note made the premier collection: the Tembo high stool and the Bolt stool. Both had been part of Marginal Notes.

Bolt was an exercise in a new, nonhierarchical way of working. 'Everyone contributed sketches. We laid them all out on the floor and took a vote.' The success of this method led Note to adopt a flat organizational structure. But because the studio hadn't developed the product based on a brief, let alone taken all 'normal' considerations into account, Bolt was designed against reason. With four legs – or 'logs', as Pigazzini calls them – the product is heavy and illogical. 'A stool with three legs is self-supporting,' he says. 'It's comical to think that something not intended for production became an award-winning stool.' (Bolt topped the Best Stool category in the Wallpaper* Design Awards 2013.)

When you develop a collection whose name evokes the jottings and doodles scribbled in the margins of a sketchpad, it's no wonder that you discover the rationality of your products only in hindsight. 'One thing Bolt's success revealed is that Marginal Notes had given us a method for our work – and that method is *no* method.' »

“Our method is *no* method

2013-2015
Greenhouse *installation*

In what we'll call 3 AD in the era of Note, the studio was asked to redesign Greenhouse, Stockholm Furniture Fair's equivalent of Milan's Salone Satellite. This section of the fair occupies historic ground. It was here that Nendo debuted in 2005 and had its first product snapped up by a manufacturer. Danish-Italian duo GamFratesi achieved the same sort of success a few years later.

For a number of years now, the fair has commissioned experienced Swedish designers to provide Greenhouse with a suitable architectural frame – a commission that runs for three years. Before Note was handed the relay baton, Taf and Jens Fager fulfilled the role, realizing elaborate schemes for the space. Taf came up with a village of small buildings with pitched roofs, and Fager mimicked the backdrop of a photo studio. Both were undoubtedly skilful exercises in exhibition architecture, but is that what Greenhouse ought to be? Pigazzini and his colleagues decided *no*. Note wanted to bring the focus back to where it belongs: young talents.

'Greenhouse allowed us to show the full gamut of our capabilities,' says Pigazzini, 'such as concept development and graphic design.' The team was adamant about not repeating the Greenhouses of the past. The plan was to shift attention to a carefully designed centrepiece at the middle of the exhibition hall. This structure functioned as a space for themed exhibitions, as well as a lounge and meeting place for visitors and exhibitors. The booths themselves 'weren't really our job', says Pigazzini, adding that they saw their centrepiece approach as something that would strengthen the Greenhouse brand and make the venue an even more attractive place for designers to show their work.

Greenhouse, a platform for young talent at Stockholm Design Week, allowed Note to show its full range of expertise – from concept development to interior and graphic design.

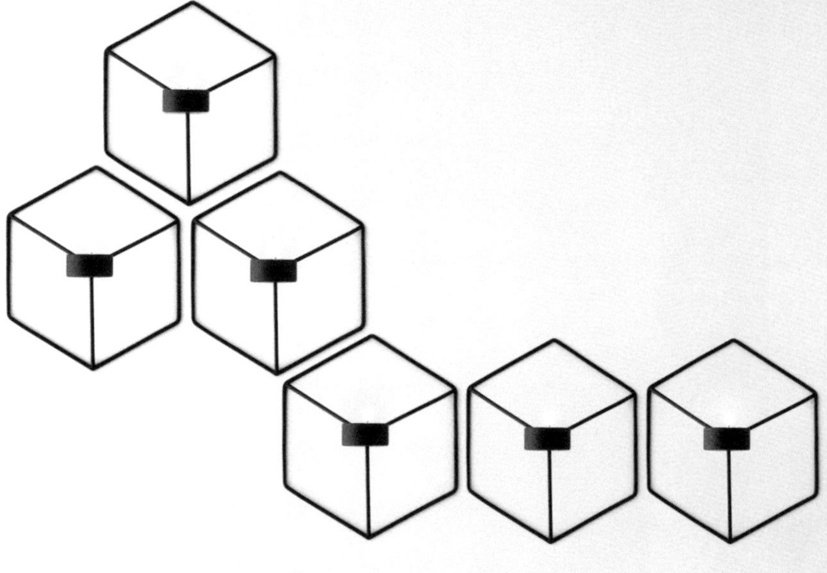

POV, a tealight holder for Danish brand Menu, is not only the studio's bestselling product but also the piece that took the least time to design.

Photo Jonas Lindström

2014
POV *candleholder*

'There's very little design in this product. The idea is so simple – it's almost nothing.' Pigazzini tells me that POV (short for Point of View), a tealight holder designed for Danish company Menu, is not only Note's bestselling product by far, but also the one that took the least time to design. He attributes its popularity to the simplicity of the object. Once the dimensions had been determined, POV was more or less done.

'It's the kind of product that makes people say: *I wonder why no one thought of this before?* It's a dream product for any company.' What's dreamlike about it – apart from a visually striking and uncomplicated appearance, which relies on a minimum of components and the use of a single material – is its slightly addictive quality. It's fun to visualize an eye-catching cluster of POVs mounted on the wall.

Again, Note had no inkling that POV would become such a big hit. The idea was presented to Menu on a whim. The lesson learned is that there's no ready-made formula for success. The designers freely admit the futility of making assumptions about what will and won't work. »

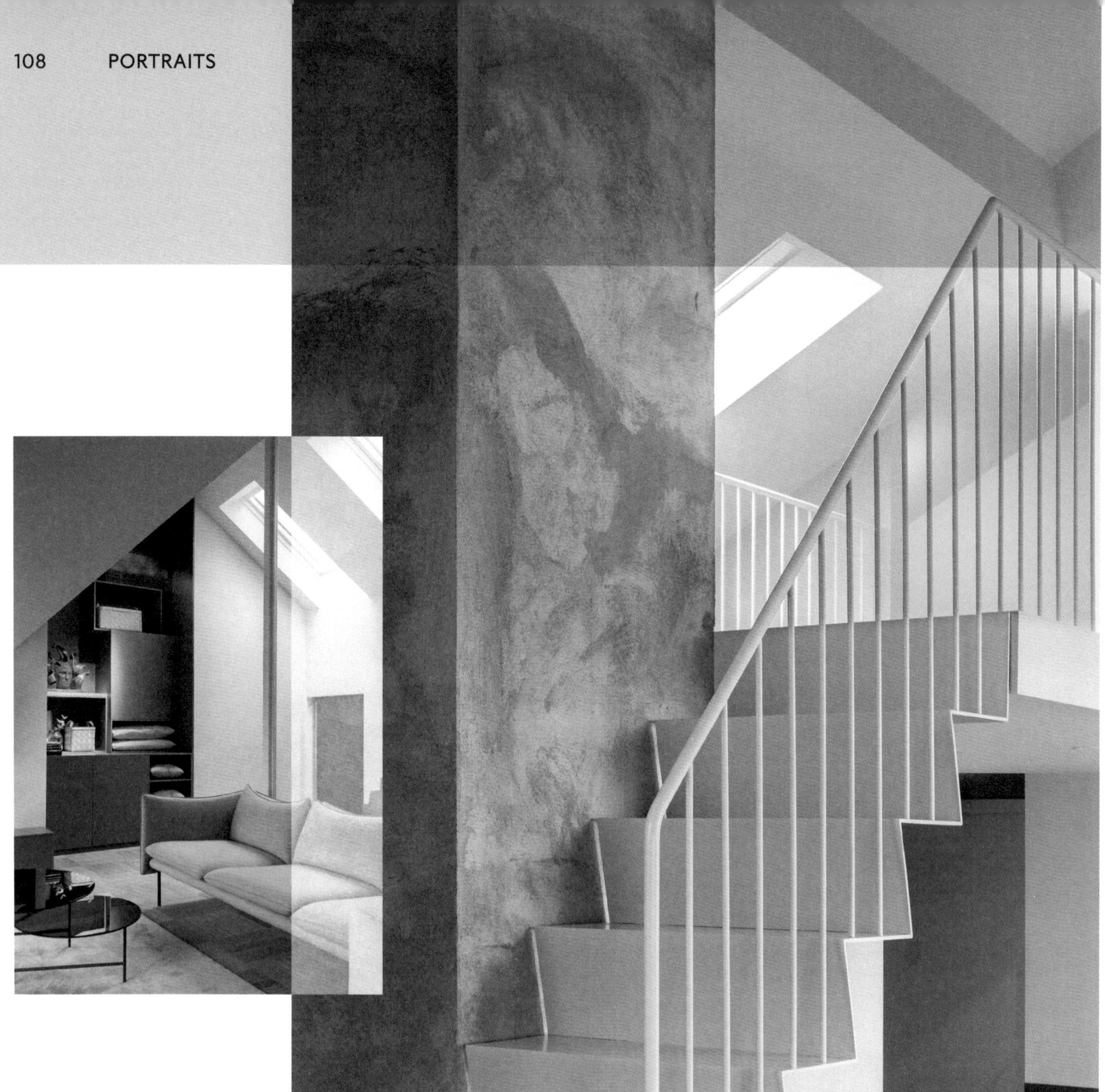

Photos courtesy of Note

Note's first residential project, the Ljungdahl apartment, allowed the team to question stereotypically Scandinavian white-on-white interior design; the project has led to further commissions for private homes.

2015 Ljungdahl *apartment*

Note's origins lie in interior design, but it wasn't until 2015 that the studio had the opportunity to test its skills on a private residence. Why was the prospect so appealing? 'We had an extremely brave client who gave us all but carte blanche,' says Pigazzini. There were some guidelines, however. The client wanted an apartment that would be welcoming and familiar, with an international flavour.

The project allowed the studio to show the entire scope of its prowess and, at the same time, to question the image of Scandinavian design. 'Isn't it funny that when you think of a Scandinavian home, the interior is entirely white?' asks Pigazzini. 'There's often no colour whatsoever on the walls. Don't you think that's a bit strange, considering how colourful Scandinavian design has become in recent years?'

Note took its 'all but carte blanche' and added colour. 'We didn't want a single white wall.' What they *did* want was pastel pink, an idea that made the client panic – 'but just a little' – at Note's initial presentation. 'We tried to show that Scandinavian design has more layers than most people think it has.' Yet again, an unconventional approach paid off. The Ljungdahl project has led to several other commissions for private residences. ●

notedesignstudio.se

GAN
DIA
BLA
SCO
75 YEARS 1941-2016
DNA design José A. Gandía-Blasco
www.gandiablasco.com
INTERIORS
FROM SPAIN
ATLANTA BARCELONA DOETINCHEM HONG KONG ISTANBUL LISBOA LOS ANGELES PORTO MADRID MIAMI NEW YORK OORDEGHEM ONTINYENT

SPACES

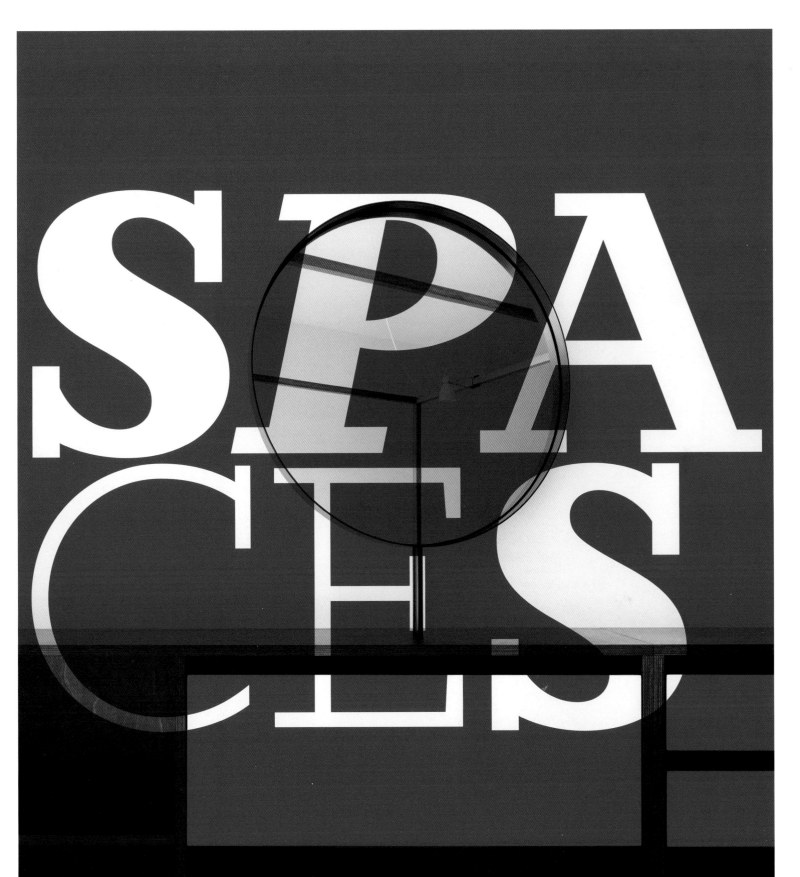

Nendo defies *department-store formulas*. Bureau Betak plants a *funhouse forest* for Dior. Dimore Studio saturates Aēsop with *colour*. Patrick Norguet gives McDonald's a *sophisticated makeover*. Neri&Hu goes *alfresco* for a Shanghai burger joint. Step inside the great indoors.

Photo Boys Play Nice

LONDON — Located on Mount Street amid late 19th-century Queen Anne revival architecture, J&M Davidson's second London boutique appears to be softy blushing: the work of Universal Design Studio, the muted interior is marked by a subdued palette of hushed white, taupe and rose, and features brushed-brass fittings and trims, radiused corners and upholstered walls.

Universal Design Studio, founded in 2001 by Edward Barber and Jay Osgerby and now co-directed by Jason Holley and Hannah Carter Owers, tinted the interior to harmonize with the brand's handbags, accessories and ready-to-wear garments. The designers framed their understated colours with crisp lines and graphic elements.

Shape, material and colour make everything heavy, yet simultaneously refined. Highlights include a cantilevering staircase to the first floor with a leather-clad banister, brushed-brass display tables reminiscent of chesspieces, a credenza with no hard edges, and a pale carpet with rounded corners embedded flush in the terrazzo floor and outlined with brass. Mirrors are alternately translucent and sharply reflective like the illumination. Meanwhile, the fitting rooms feel quietly lush: through an oversized door outlined in brass, pink leather wall panels give the impression of the most elegant quilting. — SM

universaldesignstudio.com

A subdued palette gives a **refined presence** to J&M Davidson's second London *boutique*

Photos Charles Hosea

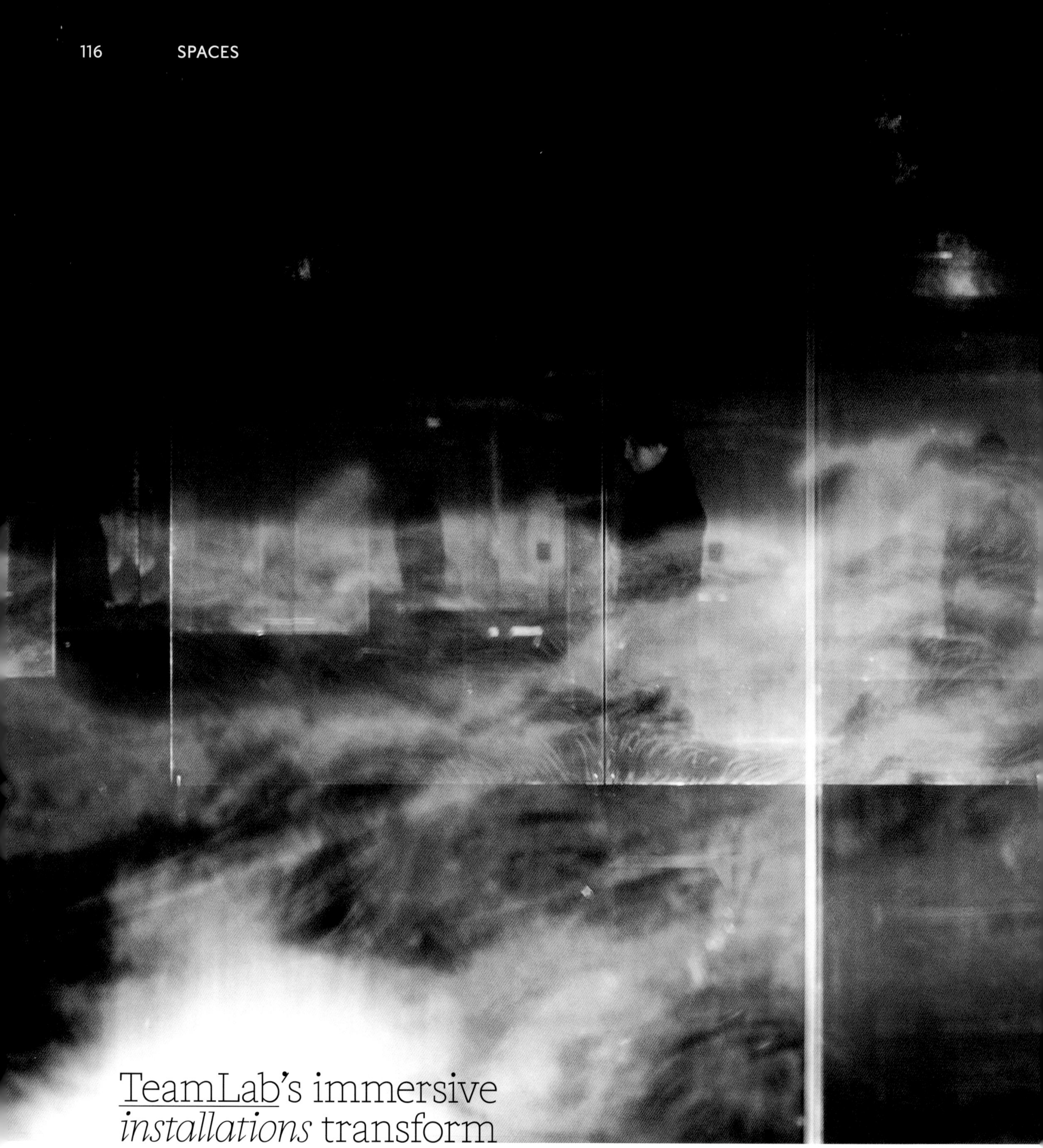

TeamLab's immersive *installations* transform natural elements into **phygital experiences**

SILICON VALLEY — As reported in *Frame* 106, Toshiyuki Inoko, director and founder of Japanese outfit TeamLab, has been challenging the boundaries that separate the physical and the digital – and dismissing the differences between art and technology – for well over two decades now. This year Inoko is taking things a step further with the presentation of his largest exhibition to date. Sweeping across a space of more than 1,850 m^2 – at Pace Gallery in Menlo Park, California, the heart of Silicon Valley – the

Explore TeamLab's immersive installations in the digital magazine

Photo courtesy of TeamLab

exhibition comprises no fewer than 20 works, many of which are appearing for the first time in North America.

Two highlights of Living Digital Space and Future Parks – the title of the show – are TeamLab's latest installations: *Light Sculpture of Flames* and *Black Waves in Infinity*. A giant cube made up of approximately 6,400 LEDs, *Light Sculpture of Flames* mimics, as the name suggests, the mesmerizing luminescence of a blazing bonfire. Suspended in midair in a darkened room, the radiant constellation of computer-generated LEDs, or 'light points', changes colour to give the illusion of flickering flames. The creation is reminiscent of a pointillist painting whose individual elements coalesce to form – in this case – an endless series of animated three-dimensional images.

Cooling things off, *Black Waves in Infinity* invites visitors to enter a sea of rough and rolling waters. Using low-tech materials such as mirrors and translucent acrylic panels, TeamLab projects images of rising and falling currents. Drawn in by the tide, gallery-goers meandering through a maze of undulating waves melt into the liquid landscape.

Strategically situated at the epicentre of the tech industry, the exhibition – which inaugurated the Pace Art + Technology program and runs until I July – hopes to generate a discussion on the role of technology in art, and vice versa. – KH

team-lab.net

Striking contrasts are at play in Hannes Peer's N°21 *flagship*

MILAN – In the heart of Milan's renowned Quadrilatero Della Moda, N°21's flagship store continues the partnership between the brand's creative director, Alessandro Dell'Acqua, and spatial designer Hannes Peer. The 150-m² shop comprises three rooms aesthetically linked by a palette of disparate materials – marble versus polycarbonate, concrete versus glass – yet separated by their distinctive interior concepts.

Reflective surfaces expand the space, while custom-made furniture creatively hones in on products: the second room, for example, sports a Damien Hirst-inspired Art Deco table sliced into six display cases – a feature also present at the brand's first outpost, in Tokyo. »

Photos Helenio Barbetta

The injection of postmodern and contemporary elements functions as a contrast to the store's historical container. In the third room, however, *ceppo di grè* – a typical Milanese stone in use almost since Roman times – makes an elegant reference to the location. Dell'Acqua calls the inclusion of this stone his 'homage to my city, Milan, and its wonderful architectural history'. Incorporated in the retail scheme is an effective background for N°21's more colourful items, as well as chic support for the brand's soberer fashions. — NB

hannespeer.com

Hannes Peer linked the three rooms of N°21's Milan flagship with a palette of disparate materials, such as marble and polycarbonate.

A spare room in Prague doubles as a **fashionably functional** *guest suite*

PRAGUE — It can be difficult to distinguish the guest room from the garage sometimes. The standard repository for spare mattresses, unloved works of art and other rejected objects deemed unfit to display elsewhere, spare rooms are generally not all that inspiring. Hospitality stakes have been raised considerably in Prague, however, where a homeowner tapped Daniel Baudis and Daniel Rohan of Ddaann to design a stylish extension for hosting family and friends.

Located on the same floor as the client's household, the compact apartment suite was designed with both comfort and privacy in mind. Close, as it were, but not overly chummy. An important consideration was to make the annexe entirely self-sufficient. On a practical level, this involved installing a kitchen and bathroom; on a design level, it meant working out a space that could be homely and yet diverting enough to ensure that visitors wouldn't feel the necessity to creep over to the main flat.

Inside, a hollow wooden framework encourages guests to focus on the optical zones between rooms. Besides serving as a welcome disruption of the tight, Bauhaus-style grid that dominates the rest of the interior, porthole-style windows create an illusion of increased space, a vital feature given the dwelling's relatively squashed dimensions.

When not in use, the extension serves as a hobby room for the lucky owner. Meanwhile, wardrobes convert into a library and storage space for bikes, a bed transforms into seating and a shower, well, a shower stays a shower whatever you do with it. — WG

ddaann.cz

Photos Boys Play Nice

Miguel Bento's *set design* at London Fashion Week has **sustainability at its core**

LONDON — In this day and age, cork isn't just for wine stoppers and kitchen floors. According to Miguel Bento, cork is the future – and not just any old future, but the best we can hope for. The set designer took part in the International Fashion Showcase, held during London Fashion Week. The theme was Utopia, specially chosen to commemorate the anniversary of Thomas More's seminal treatise of the same name, which hit the medieval shelves 500 years ago. Countries from all around the world were invited to contribute, including Bento's native Portugal.

Bento translated More's vision into one word for the 21st century: sustainability. Okay, two words: sustainability and cork. It turns out that cork is a wonderful material. Not only is zero waste created during production, as only the bark of the tree is used to make it; cork is also completely renewable.

Instead of embracing cork's soft, tree-hugging character, however, Bento showed off its more industrial, aggressive side. He built a giant structure out of robust blocks of the stuff supplied by Amorim Cork. Deliberately avoiding the familiar organic-brown hue associated with cork, he crafted what appeared to be angular boulders of granite and marble. It's only the odd glimpse of traditional cork that gave the game away. Visitors strolling through the brutalism-inspired installation could admire clothing from five emerging Portuguese designers, who will be hoping for another kind of sustainability: that of the growth variety. — WG

mbento.com

Photos Nian Canard

Modern insertions serve as **connective tissue** at a *co-working space* in Brooklyn

BROOKLYN — Owing to budget-induced, 19th-century design flaws, the Gowanus Canal in Brooklyn, New York, used to stink. Its water didn't even contain enough oxygen to sustain life. In a sharp turnabout, creative studios are now breathing new life into the neighbourhood.

To wit: the opening of work-share space Coworkrs, which offers 24/7 access to offices (and a kitchen stocked with

Photo courtesy of Leeser Architecture

beer on tap). This is not your grandma's conventional workspace. Over three floors and 4,330 m², Coworkrs serves sundry creatives, not-for-profits and tech start-ups with radically diverse needs.

To offset the variance of private offices, Dumbo-based Leeser Architecture designed, among other things, robust communal space. Quite dramatically, Leeser dovetailed the historical timber, concrete and brick factory with modern insertions – most notably an origami-like metal stairwell enclosure – that serve as 'connective tissue' for both the building and the community inside. The other unifying element is colour, which is used to signify 'object, motion and stasis': Yves Klein blue for the sculptural stair enclosure, teal for its interior and circulation, and glacial blue for lounges and other rest areas.

'The trend towards co-working spaces is only the beginning of an evolving hybridization of work and living spaces,' says Thomas Leeser. 'In the future, our workspaces will include residential components, micro-farming, childcare and education, as well as a growing maker industry spurred on by the 3D-printing revolution.' – SM

leeser.com

Bureau Betak **distorts and refracts reality** at a *runway show* in Paris

PARIS — Alexandre de Betak has done everyone in the fashion industry, from Hussein Chalayan to Sies Marjan. And by 'done' we mean he designed their catwalks. For more than one Christian Dior *défilé*, Bureau Betak used bushels and bushels of flowers (*Frame* 108, p. 82). This January, however, to showcase the House of Dior's S/S 2016 couture collection, the team opted for 1,500 m^2 of mirror panels, each made from a light, highly reflective, technically specified film stretched over an aluminium frame.

Planted in the garden of Paris's recently renovated Musée Rodin, the exterior of the circular looking-glass pavilion was dressed in 12-m-high pleated panels that reflected the museum's aristocratic rear façade, the colourful arrival of guests and the shifting skies above. Inside, images of wooden floors appeared in both mirrored ceiling and walls: 40 mirrors were arranged around the perimeter and 15 placed in the centre of the room in sets of two, three or four panels, depending on the desired shape.

Forming two concentric pleated rings with all the mysterious beauty of a funhouse forest, accordions of mirrors strategically placed among the spectators' cobalt benches did nothing to impede the circulation of models moving through the space. The angles of these folds were determined by their ability to reflect one another while generating a kaleidoscopic effect as the models walked, abstracting everything around them into, one might say, melting bouquets of bright blue flowers. — SM

bureaubetak.com

Photos Nicolas Du Pasquier, courtesy of Bureau Betak

At Hermès, fanciful *window installations* **seduce sans merchandise**

TOKYO — Mysterious bodies infiltrated the display window of a Hermès store in Tokyo's Ginza district this spring, arousing the curiosity of commuters and *flâneurs* as they passed. The outlandish installation – aptly titled *Incursion* – was the creation of British artist and sculptor Kate MccGwire, whose admiration for the natural world is evidenced by her work: in lieu of traditional materials such as marble

Photo Satoshi Asakawa, courtesy of Hermès

or stone, McCGwire works almost exclusively with bird feathers. Using plumage collected from farmers and gamekeepers, she endows the ordinary with an otherworldly character. The resulting feathery forms are at once mesmerizing and grotesque.

Inspired by the Hermès 2016 campaign, Nature at Full Gallop, McCGwire's sculptures attracted passers-by with their iridescent gleam and sensuous curves. The undulating forms engulfed the windows with an oozing lifelike presence, bringing a dreamy quality to the otherwise static world. Glistening under the glow of spotlights, the fluid forms bore a strange likeness to sunbathing sea lions. In one window, a table, a gentleman's shoe and silverware lay scattered about as if to suggest a sudden commotion. Did a monster break in and drive away the inhabitant? Or did the occupant become the monster? Bizarre creatures and scenes aside, adding to the level of eeriness was the noticeable absence of products on display. Another example of storytelling as *the* retail strategy of the future? — KH

katemccgwire.com

Visitors to a *nail parlour* in Mexico get swept away by a cascading **parade of colour**

ZAPOPAN — Nail It beauty bar recently opened the doors to its second location in Zapopan, Mexico. Designed by Guadalajara-based outfit Estudio Ala, the nail salon's open-plan interior is divided into two visual strata. At eye level, the 85-m² floor is completely white, seamed only slightly by the crisp forms of its pearly furnishings. Overhead, coloured rods rain from the ceiling in a saturated *ombre* of pink, purple, aquamarine and blue that appears to shift as one passes.

No fewer than 7,000 recycled broomsticks – all damaged during production – were mounted on the ceiling using eyebolts at 8-mm intervals, which fasten the sticks to OSB panels. Underneath, the whiteness serves as a blank backdrop against which clients are under no external influence to select polish colours and nail art.

Estudio Ala's designs are site-specific, but also universally accessible. Here, they create a thirst for colour in clients, guiding them through a vast palette of options while leaving room to pick the perfect varnish from among them. The designers chose four ceiling colours that start with warm pink and move into cooler hues. 'We wanted to avoid colour stereotypes,' explains industrial designer Armida Fernández, who founded the multidisciplinary studio with architect Luis Enrique Flores. 'The associations depend on the context, the use of space and the story transmitted by the concept. We wanted to speak of something extremely universal and powerful.' – SM

estudioala.com

Photos César Béjar

NAIL IT

Doshi Levien's *stand* quite literally **rolls out Bolon's new campaign** during Stockholm Design Week

Photos courtesy of Bolon

STOCKHOLM — 'We wanted to create desirability around the material,' says Nipa Doshi of London-based studio Doshi Levien (see page 78), which she cofounded with partner Jonathan Levien. Her words refer to the Stockholm Furniture & Light Fair stand the couple designed for Swedish flooring brand Bolon. The stand — the duo prefers the term 'installation' — is part of a much bigger campaign, which introduces Bolon By You, a collection that includes the option of customized flooring. Doshi Levien is

responsible for the entire project, which entails everything from curating the brand's visual identity to consulting on colours for the flooring series. The campaign launch featured at the fair in Stockholm.

A wavy wall guided visitors along small seating areas. 'The mazelike formation of the installation really invited people in,' says Levien. 'It created a connection between visitors and product, as they moved through and touched the different patterns.' The layout of the stand also reflected how the collection is made. 'We wanted to emphasize the fact that this floor is like a textile,' he continues. 'The material is woven on a Jacquard loom, which produces a seemingly endless roll of carpeting.' Doshi Levien took that roll, stood it upright, and the idea for the stand was born.

Appearing on the uninterrupted surface of the undulating wall are various graphic collages, which the designers call 'material interventions'. 'Our first response to the Bolon weaves was to combine them with materials like wood, metal and marble,' says Levien. 'In Stockholm we wanted visiting architects to envisage the product in conjunction with other architectural materials.' He and Doshi poetically communicated the versatility of the collection in an intriguing setting not easily forgotten. — FK

doshilevien.com

Three *showrooms*, **three moods, one building**: Zemberek Design shows off the many sides of Skechers

ISTANBUL — When hired to design the six-storey Istanbul headquarters for the Turkish distributor of international footwear giant Skechers, Zemberek Design was tasked with realizing heterogeneity within a homogenous brand space. The resulting interiors reinforce brand identity while accommodating a rotating range of Skechers' 3,500 seasonal products across three dedicated footwear showrooms: Performance, Casual and Kids. 'We thought that a single showroom concept containing all products would be boring,' says Zemberek partner Başak Emrence. 'We didn't want customers to have a tiresome, time-consuming experience.'

The team established distinct ecosystems within a larger biosphere. All spaces share some materials – such as metals, black fabrics and concrete-like plaster – as well as curvilinear forms. In each functional zone (reception, offices and discrete showrooms), however, metals and plaster have diverse finishes, fabrics are used in different ways, and the resulting structures vary as well.

On the reception and meeting level, fabric stretches between CNC-milled steel frames that camber between floor and ceiling. Bisecting the building diagonally, these frames create walls that cant and flex elastically like billowing drapery, while looking as robust as canyon walls and drawing visitors from a dark, intimate entrance towards a bright meeting room.

In the Performance showroom, a display made of dark steel and fabric wraps perimeter walls. Holding shelves »

Photos Şafak Emrence

that step back as they rise towards the ceiling, the display assumes a supple, dynamic form that communicates comfort, flexibility and fluid movement.

The mesh textile common to footwear appears to be scaled up in the Casual showroom, where Zemberek installed semipermeable display walls. Individual fold-down shelves of iroko wood are hinged to the solid perimeter walls or anchored on gridded frames of varnished raw steel. When a shelf is empty, it folds into the wall. It either becomes part of a graphic pattern against a solid wall or closes up a square in the grid of partition frames – a space that reopens when the shelf folds down to hold a shoe.

For the Kids showroom, 'we dug into our childhood memories', says Şafak Emrence. The designers applied their recollections in a grown-up fashion, using metal-mesh shelving in geometric shapes, Plexiglas and painted wood to evoke sweets, Ferris wheels and playtime. Here, and throughout the space, products remain in the foreground. – SM

zemberek.org

In the Kids showroom at Skechers Istanbul, Zemberek evoked sweets, Ferris wheels and playtime.

BURGER SPOT

Neri&Hu **emancipates the interior** of a Shanghai *burger joint*

SHANGHAI — Neri&Hu hits another home(town) run with Rachel's, a restaurant that brings the 1950s American burger-joint vibe to Shanghai. In a city known for its hot, humid summers, the designers intentionally allowed the architecture to spill out into the street by incorporating a façade that opens up to merge interior and exterior.

Not only does the concept give patrons a taste of the outdoors; it also gives the illusion of extra space in one of China's most densely populated cities. When the folding façade is sealed shut, glass and mirror fulfil the space-stretching role, bouncing both light and views of the surrounding streetscape into the 93-m^2 interior. The open-air feel extends to the ceiling, where skylights add a sense of weightlessness to the structure.

In what's becoming a Neri&Hu signature, flooring moves up to form furniture elements. Here, hand-painted tiles are both underfoot and under table, serving as the bases of custom-designed dining stations. Complete with pivoting bases made from steel, seating can swing this way or that to accommodate groups of various numbers. — TI

en.neriandhu.com

Photos Dirk Weiblen

A *trading centre* in China uses **data as digital wallpaper**

XI'AN — To match its multibillion-yuan investment in developing Midwest Inland Port Financial Town — the largest metal-trading platform in Asia to date — Maike Metals Group needed a sizable gesture. The international bid for the project in Xi'an, China, was awarded to Shenzen-based Hallucinate, whose design transforms data into a graphic spatial element.

The designers incorporated digital walls — a modern-day play on ticker tape — to 'blur the boundaries between reality and imagination, modern technology and architecture'. Clad in lengths of customized extruded aluminium, the walls incorporate LED displays. A translucent coating softens the effect, making the displays more appealing to the eye. The panelled structure also helps to absorb sound in the large, open lobby.

Rather than let the exterior determine the layout inside, Hallucinate fashioned what it calls an 'interior façade' from the ticker-tape structure. The designers say they adopted this approach as it allows for undisrupted views from floor to ceiling. — TI

hallucinate.com.cn

Photos Javier Callejas Sevilla

McDonald's ditches *fast-food-chain* clichés to **update its image** in Paris

PARIS — The refurbished McDonald's Champs-Élysées is a far cry from an eatery brandishing vinyl-covered booths and chipped laminate. Patrick Norguet's sophisticated interior for the two-storey flagship reflects the sizable shift that McDonald's France is making towards quality produce and sustainable agriculture.

Norguet's previous work with *le McDo* on concept designs for its French stores gave him the opportunity to push the new image into 'radically modern' territory. He approached the bespoke project by putting the customer first and drawing inspiration from new offerings and technologies – including table service, touchscreens and tablets – now available at the location.

While recognizing that withstanding the site's heavy traffic was a priority, Norguet also wanted to inject intimacy into the dining area: pendant lighting is kept at 'nonaggressive' levels and acoustic ceiling panels manage noise. Playing off transparency and perforation, he used a simple yet strong mix of glass, metal-mesh screens and raw concrete. Pared-back materials contrast with details such as etched typography on the walls and a colourful tunnel of light boxes at the upper level, which display photography by SND and artist Frank Hülsbömer. Fittings and furnishings from the likes of Artemide, Arper, Alias and Kristalia demonstrate how much Norguet relishes bringing quality design to unexpected settings. 'Even if it's fast food, we can still take the time to share a nice moment.' — JDP

patricknorguet.com

Photos Renaud Callebaut

SEATTLE — San Francisco isn't the only US city whose urban fabric is undergoing transformation thanks to the influx of tech companies. Up the coast in Seattle, professionals are arriving in droves to meet the industry's needs, and gentrification is well afoot. The scenario has prompted entrepreneurs to realize new spaces in the city, and younger firms like Best Practice are eager to supply the demand for designers. Eye Eye, an optometrist and eyewear store in Capitol Hill, highlights Best Practice's position in the market. The studio places its work 'outside of the regular sphere in Seattle', says Kailin Gregga. She explains that 'the city once had a locally focused design aesthetic with an emphasis on natural materials and handicraft'. Let's call it the 'hipster look', which was exported the world over. Gregga says that while Best Practice is 'committed to working with local materials and manufacturers, we seek to express them in a more conceptual fashion. We're more interested in providing dynamic experiences and surprises than in appealing to a particular aesthetic. In a world that fetishizes timber, blackened steel and concrete, we're not afraid to use different materials or colour.'

Surprise comes in the form of mirrors that toy with perception – just as a pair of glasses does. Mirrors in the blue house-like structure also fulfil a functional role, allowing shoppers to see their bespectacled selves from different angles. — TI
bestpracticearchitecture.com

Best Practice's *optometrist* and *eyewear store* **eschews Seattle stereotypes**

Photos Rafael Soldi

With a new *store* in Paris, Paco Rabanne **stimulates the senses** for an evocative retail experience

PARIS — Over a decade has passed since Paco Rabanne opened its first and only Parisian flagship store. It was with great anticipation, therefore, that the brand announced the inauguration of its second location – a stone's throw from Place Vendôme and Coco Chanel's legendary hat boutique and apartment – in the capital's 1st arrondissement. Its gleaming façade of glass and perforated metal greets visitors to the shop at Rue Cambon 12.

A design by Belgian architecture firm Office Kersten Geers David Van Severen, the shop's striking aluminium metalwork – which is carried through to the interior – is softened by a constellation of nude leather floor tiles. Occupying 65 m^2, the retail space is dictated by a juxtaposition of 'intimate and exhibitionist interventions': a hybrid display-cum-storage unit and a system of semitransparent elements that exhibit the brand's garments and accessories without giving too much away. Small openings, or 'windows', provide a glimpse of what's inside. Aimed at deepening the relationship between fashion and architecture, the interior design incorporates a dichotomy between 'openness and complete enclosure'.

Adding an extra dose of sophistication to the shop, a custom-made fragrance by renowned perfumer Dominique Ropion and abstract electronic music by Benoit Heitz, alias Surkin, set the aroma and mood for an undeniably refined shopping experience. — MM

officekgdvs.com

Photos Jean-Etienne Portail

Photo Raimond Wouda

Jeroen Kooijmans' immersive *installation* addresses **fanaticism, mania and war**

DEN BOSCH — *The Fish Pond Song* – a video work by Jeroen Kooijmans at the Stedelijk Museum 's-Hertogenbosch in the Netherlands – guides visitors through an imaginary world of war, propelled by narratives of fear, dreams and lust. Exhibited in its entirety for the first time, the more than 700-m^2 installation unfolds over three chapters, communicating war as an abstract reality – a lurking evil and psychological madness.

Kooijmans has been known to reference the often religious-themed work of medieval Dutch painter Hieronymus Bosch. *The Fish Pond Song* is no exception; here, the artist draws on *The Garden of Earthly Delights*. Kooijmans' work deals with the topic of faith in relation to the 2001 attacks on the Twin Towers. He tackles such themes as fanaticism, mania and war.

Video projections featured in the spatial installation appear on simple archetypal structures and their surrounding walls – not unlike the set for a contemporary theatre performance. Compared with the voyeuristic distance often offered in a playhouse, *The Fish Pond Song* allows visitors to immerse themselves fully in the projected landscapes and to more actively engage in their thought-provoking content. – JP

***The Fish Pond Song* is on show at Stedelijk Museum 's-Hertogenbosch until 5 June 2016**
jeroenkooijmans.com

After a string of *retail spaces* in neutral colours, Aēsop **goes bold in deep green** on Corso Magenta

MILAN — A few months after opening its first Milan outpost on Via Meravigli, Aēsop doubled up with a second. Located on Corso Magenta and just a ten-minute walk from the original store, the Dimore Studio-designed space conveys the Australian skincare brand's classic-meets-modern image. It's a look well suited to Italy's most fashion-conscious, forward-thinking city.

The designers say the idea was to pull in materials typically used in the butler's pantries of large 1930s Italian villas, such as linoleum floors, Formica countertops, square ceramic tiles and ribbed glass. The Milan-based firm, founded by Britt Moran and Emiliano Salci, is versed in blending antiquity with modernity. At Aēsop, the goal was to transform the selection of materials into 'a contemporary version of the small neighbourhood *bottega* still so common in the vicinity of Corso Magenta'.

Many of Aēsop's recent offerings have been decidedly neutral in colour, but its latest retail interior is a sea of deep green. Display cases feature rounded corners that soften the overall aesthetic, while pastel tones serve as a backdrop, allowing the products to pop out in an effective yet unaggressive way. Two large discs suspended from a canopy of brass rods shed a diffused light throughout the space.

The result is an ideal translation of Aēsop in the context of post-expo Milan, a place where projects like Wes Anderson's Bar Luce at Fondazione Prada (*Frame* 106, p. 120) have managed to balance the city's elegance with its industrious drive for innovation. — NB

dimorestudio.eu

Photos Paola Pansini

A *nightclub* in Bulgaria sends visitors deeper **down the rabbit hole**

SOFIA — Many spatial designers have invoked the whimsy of *Alice in Wonderland*, but Svetoslav Todorov of Studio Mode set out to 'find out how deep the rabbit hole goes' at Club Mascara. In the Bulgarian city of Sofia, Mode devised what it refers to as the 'missing chapter' of the book. 'Everyone is both actor and spectator, the DJ is the director, Mode is the composer, and Mascara is the grand scene.'

Mode's monochromatic approach plays with the perception of black and white, light and dark – a theme extracted from Lewis Carroll's book. Contrast, therefore, takes the lead. The fluid lines of curved white wainscoting meet sharp angles on floor and ceiling, where triangular tiles below are mimicked in the structure above. Separated from the general area by the central bar, the dimly lit VIP zone is suffused with darker shades.

The club's theatricality pairs perfectly with the site: the basement level of the National Opera and Ballet. Operatic decor, scenography and costumes served as further inspiration for Mode. 'Each motif and detail is designed to distort imagination and perception.' — TI

studiomode.eu

Photo Tihomir Rachev

TOKYO — When tasked with updating the women's fashion area of Japanese department store Seibu Shibuya, Nendo opted for an amusement-park theme that would appeal to the younger woman. Eschewing the prevailing department-store formula – in which each fashion label has an individually designed retail space in sync with its brand identity – the Key to Style area has no distinct lines separating labels from one another. To unify the floor, Nendo treated each brand as an equal in the scheme.

The 1047-m² space is envisioned as an *en plein air* fairground that invites shoppers to peruse fashions in settings reminiscent of market stalls and wagons. Lambrequin motifs dress the ceiling, »

Nendo gives *department-store* shopping a **carnival twist**

Photos Takumi Ota

adding a festive, circus-like vibe. Retail zones are marked by parquet flooring with pattern-free paths that help guide shoppers and maintain flow.

Nendo was also responsible for renovating the hats section on the floor below. Unlike the open-air ambience of the women's area, this retail space is tucked away in a corner. To usher shoppers into the secluded spot, Nendo went for a touch of pink, which distinguishes the department from its rather conservatively coloured surroundings. True to playful form, the designer conjured a cloud of 120 odd hats that mimic umbrellas when perched on their display arms.

The curvature of the walls corresponds to a ceiling that features large hovering discs, which provide illumination and represent clouds in the sky, reinforcing Nendo's concept of outdoor fun. — KH
nendo.jp

Quirky display arms make hats resemble umbrellas in Nendo's intervention at Tokyo's Seibu Shibuya department store.

wetransfer.com

Retail LAB

Brands on Show

The rapid rise of e-commerce means that retailers can no longer afford to ignore opportunities outside the traditional store environment. Brands are starting to *provide content* that supports the products they sell. From *pop-up exhibitions* to *workshops*, this issue's Frame Lab reveals how retailers are *branching out* to reel in the crowds and *increase their fandom*.

Photo Vincent van Gurp

Fashion

Photos Mark Blower

Fandoms

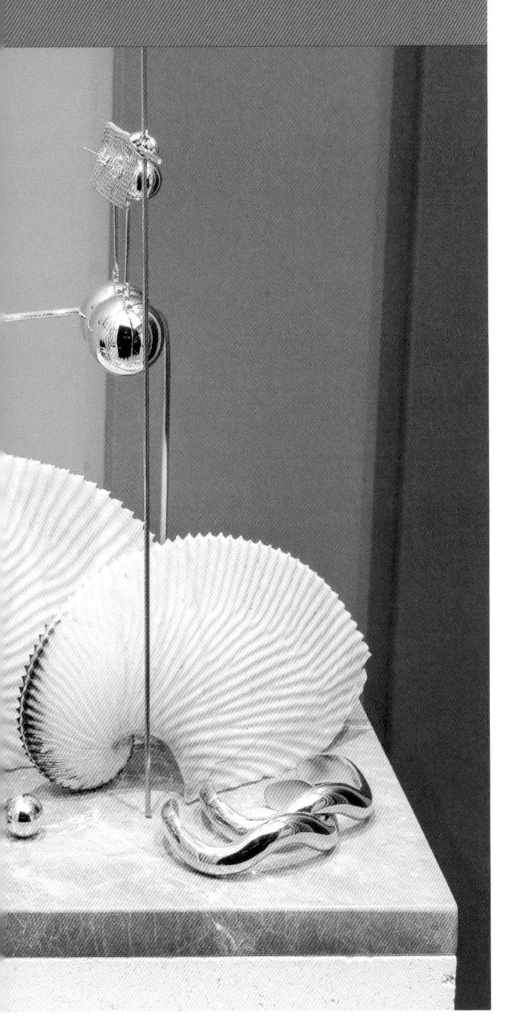

From ***curated exhibitions*** **to** ***engrossing brandscapes*****, Bradley Quinn investigates what's in store for fashion retail.**

Words **Bradley Quinn**

Instead of opening a flagship store, J.W.Anderson CEO Jonathan Anderson launched a workshop for collaborations between his brand and various makers. The results of their joint efforts will have to compete, however, with the interior's intensely coloured walls.

Fresh approaches to brand design reconfigure the retail landscape in exciting new ways. Consumer engagement is still key, but brands are distracting customers from their digital devices and channelling attention towards real-world experiences. The consumer's growing expectation of personalized encounters is being swapped for expressions of brand personality, sparking a shift from retail theatricalities to honest manifestations of authenticity. While the demand for responsive, tech-fuelled hotspots may motivate many consumers to step over the retail threshold, some labels are luring customers into branded environments where low-tech stories are told. Brand storytelling remains potent in appeal, engaging audiences in ways that may be more meaningful than digital storylines alone.

While the future of retail is undoubtedly high-tech, some of the most compelling concepts emerging today are those in which technology takes a backseat. From community-building initiatives and curated shows to lifestyle services and sporting arenas, brands are creating social experiences that embrace whole demographics rather than targeting individual tribes. As omni-channel retail streams extend their reach, some brands infiltrate dating apps and so-called hook-up hangouts, while others forge alliances with the travel and hospitality sectors to generate innovative opportunities for shopping. Reaching consumers in places that they know and trust breaks down brick-and-mortar barriers and bridges the digital divide, seamlessly integrating retail and everyday life.

Curating: The New Merchandising?

Retail storylines often highlight aspects of brands and products that consumers may have missed – or overlay a narrative that engages a wider audience. This strategy reveals how retail is becoming increasingly editorialized, feeding consumers' hunger for insider information and behind-the-scenes knowledge. With editorial streams emerging in both physical and digital platforms, brands are extending their reach by becoming content providers, offering more than products and services alone.

Luxury fashion labels are cashing in on the cultural cache associated with museum and gallery presentations, providing compelling content for exhibitions and events. Big-brand fashion exhibitions are nothing new; luxury retailers such as Louis Vuitton, Hermès, Gucci and Bottega Veneta even have their own galleries. Last autumn, Chanel teamed up with London's Saatchi Gallery to produce the Mademoiselle Privé exhibition. »

McQ's London flagship has a basement gallery that articulates the label's commitment to art and, in so doing, adds a new element to the existing brand narrative.

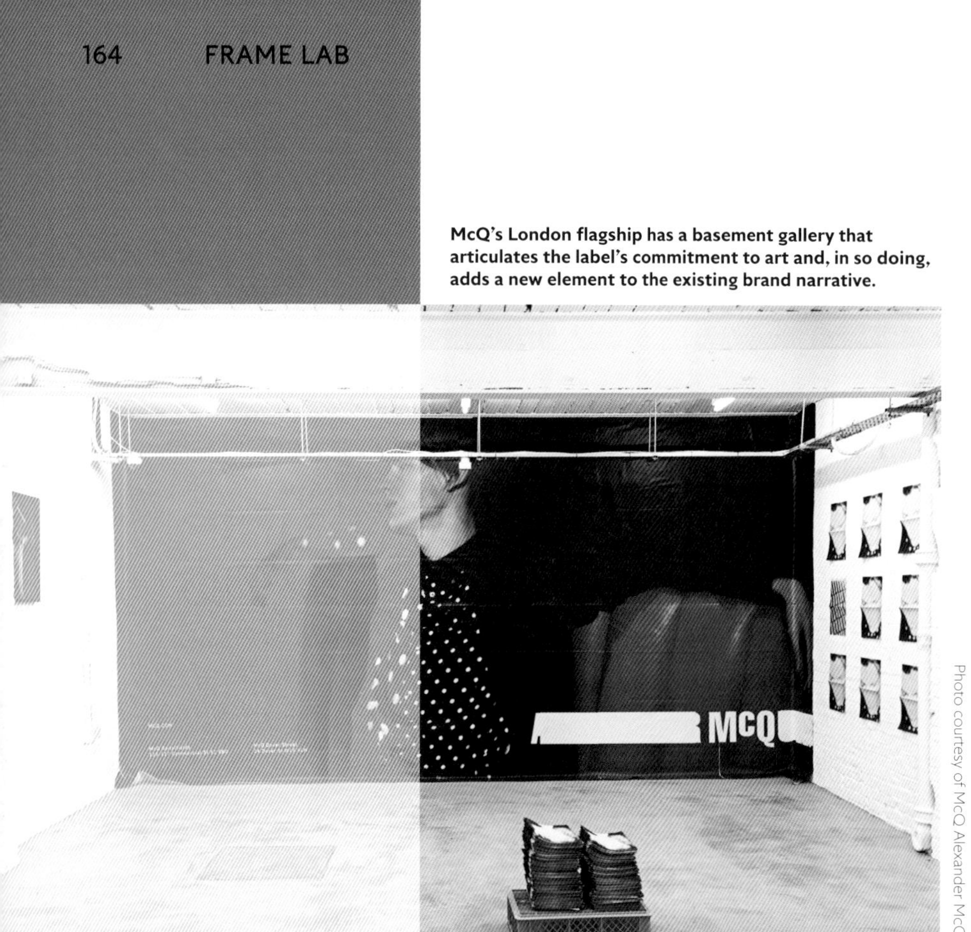

Photo courtesy of McQ Alexander McQueen

A curated overview of the brand's history, it was meant to provide insight into the 'irreverent' and perhaps eccentric personalities of Madame Chanel and Karl Lagerfeld. The decision to partner with the Saatchi was a shrewd one, as the gallery is associated with established art stars around the world and is a destination for couture-buying lovers of contemporary art. Mademoiselle Privé showcased garments and graphics from different chapters of the brand's story, recounting Chanel's history with narratives that made the fashion house seem very 21st century.

Louis Vuitton is also on the gallery circuit, with the Series 3 exhibition (*Frame* 108, p. 098) landing in London after Series 1 appeared in Tokyo and Shanghai and Series 2 in LA, Beijing, Seoul and Rome. LV's latest exhibition at the Grand Palais in Paris – Volez, Voguez, Voyagez – displayed vintage trunks, contemporary *prêt-à-porter* and classic leather goods. The exhibition's remit was to decode the brand's history and launch a new vision of its past, present and future. It's easier for brands to explore historical narratives through exhibitions than with retail operations. Space on the shop floor is reserved for products for sale now, with little room left over for sequential storytelling. The exhibition format is a favourite of heritage brands, who use it to acquaint customers with their legacy and longevity: insider knowledge that consumers don't normally have access to when they shop.

“Consumers assume that brands can reach them on all retail streams

When Alexander McQueen's lower-priced diffusion line, McQ, opened its flagship shop in London last autumn, the brand included a gallery space in the basement. The gallery articulates the brand's commitment to art through a rotating exhibition programme that showcases young artists. As customers descend into the gallery, they will likely encounter narratives that amplify McQ's cool, edgy messages. Already a destination in itself, the basement space traffics art-world consumers into the store who may have missed it otherwise.

Also based in London, the J.W.Anderson brand is skyrocketing in popularity yet prefers to maintain a low profile. In an interview with businessoffashion.com earlier this year, CEO Jonathan Anderson says he turned down an opportunity to open a showroom and flagship shop in a prime retail location. For Anderson, the brand message is a cultural one that invites participation and interaction rather than just showing off products. Anderson announced the launch of the Jonathan Anderson Workshops, a project inspired by the Bloomsbury Group's Omega Workshops established in 1913. Anderson wants to personalize his customers' relationship with the brand by sharing knowledge, ideas, insights and inspiration. He plans to involve artists, musicians and other cultural figures in the curation of a programme of experiences, which he favours over retail representation.

When retail units contain art galleries, bookstores and cafés, consumers can begin to sense everything the brand stands for. Such spaces add a lifestyle dimension that introduces new elements to existing brand narratives, potentially transcending conventional retail as they extend brand messages across a range of platforms.

Brandscaping

A bigger concept of brand design is emerging, so broad that it defies conventional space. Whereas traditional retail concepts seem limited, the potential to reach consumers through lifestyle-related activities is infinite. Nike (see page 169) famously opened a temporary skate park in Brooklyn, New York, where boarders and Nike fans were welcome to try new products and apps. Nike also took its edgy branding to downtown Manhattan, where a new showroom and fitness studio occupy a former metalwork shop. Nike uses the fitness studio to introduce celebrities, athletes and VIPs to new products in a high-energy environment where they can put them to the test.

Meeting consumers on their own turf or inviting them to brandscaped spaces leads to new kinds of interactions. Real stories result as consumers mentally shift from a state of 'getting' to one of 'being' and come away with experiences beyond those that can be gained on a typical shopping trip. Sports-related brandscapes take consumers away from glossy brand presentations and immerse them in dynamic environments, where surging adrenaline and pounding heartbeats become part of the product soon after it's held or fitted on for the first time.

British cycle brand Rapha opened a climate-controlled studio where customers can try on garments and test them on a stationary bike that even lets them select the force of the headwind they want to face. Consumers receive insider information during the trial as they learn how »

Retail Futures

Five tendencies that promise to enhance the shopping experience

OMNI-CHANNEL EXPANSION

Just as the Internet of Things is creating new digital markets, inter-channel schemes aim to connect with services that consumers rely on. Expect fashion to find footholds in retail banking, hospitality, healthcare, education, and the automotive and aerospace industries.

CONCIERGE CONSUMPTION

Brands can build relationships by exposing consumers to products that reflect individual preferences. The bespoke approach is enhanced by tracking apps that give brands up-to-date information about the consumer.

HYPER-RETAIL

As retail moves beyond traditional boundaries, digital tools will enhance the shop-ability of the world around us. The use of 3D scanning technology will allow us to identify garments and accessories that appear in videos, at events and in public space, while superimposing a 'buy' button onto any item recognized.

ROVING RETAIL

Fashion brands are on the move, selling their products via pop-up shops, drive-thru vending and trunk shows. Roving retail not only catches consumers found outside traditional brand spaces, but also has the potential to provide hotspots for tech-fuelled connections.

BRAND BATTLEGROUNDS

Today's fashion labels are competing in entirely new arenas, where public space, utopian bodies, the quality of the experience and the all-pervasive reach of retail are forging new frontiers. As brands struggle to understand these new platforms, they will clash as they compete for emerging markets.

Visitors to the Marni Flower Café on the third floor of the Umeda Hankyu Department Store in Osaka are pampered by the fashion label's offering of Italian specialities, customized products and flowers.

Photo courtesy of Marni

stationary bikes are central to the brand's product development and testing standards. In January, fast fashion brand H&M hosted a pop-up fitness studio in Warsaw, where consumers exercised to 'earn' garments from H&M's new sportswear collection. The brand plugged into the fitness frenzy triggered at the beginning of the new year in order to forge stronger connections with sporty audiences.

At its best, brandscaping parallels developments in e-commerce and embraces digital lifestyles. Fashion retailers are beginning to understand that consumers assume a scenario in which brands can reach them on all retail streams and even detect the moments when new clothing is needed most. Aware of this expectation, Gap converged with concierge services at selected Virgin Hotels that now stock Gap's basics range and deliver products directly to the rooms. Guests who forget essential items or need new clothing before they leave the hotel can order them from the concierge: it's just another aspect of room service.

San Francisco-based fashion e-tailer Everlane partnered with boutique hotels in four American cities, bringing its products offline and into luxury environments. Everlane takes over expensive suites and invites guests to try the latest products, hoping to win new customers offline. Such promotions reinforce the message that Everlane's products travel to consumers, and not the other way round. A smart move, as clients staying in high-end hotels are likelier to spend more on fashion and accessories than budget travellers do.

Brands are extending their reach by becoming content providers, offering more than products and services alone

S-Commerce

Social-media streams and the sales opportunities they lead to are important parts of a brand's ecosystem. Social-media platforms that are attuned to millennial mind-sets include messaging apps, video, built-in VR and AR capabilities, and shareable wish lists. While such platforms can facilitate e-commerce to the point of making online transactions a seamless part of the process, they may unwittingly distance consumers from the authenticity that brands strive to project. The appeal of brandscaped spaces and interactive workshops lies in their capacity to unite consumers by involving them in a group dynamic, effectively storytelling in real time to foster perceptions of authenticity.

Some brands are pioneering new approaches to retail through 's-commerce' initiatives that galvanize consumers to pay attention to humanistic concerns. During the 2015 holiday season, Gap teamed up with sock brand Bombas to encourage 'good deeds' by giving away socks to people in need. After Bombas discovered that socks were the most requested item in homeless shelters, the company developed special products with reinforced seams, antimicrobial fibres and darker colours, which minimize visible wear. Designed with the homeless in mind, the socks made a difference to those unable to put on a fresh pair every day.

The partnership with Bombas was part of Gap's ongoing commitment to support local communities. Both brands promoted the initiative through social media; their hashtag was #socksforall. During the campaign, window displays in Gap's Fifth Avenue flagship featured a towering 'Good Deed Machine' created by local art studio Red Paper Heart. Passers-by saw signs encouraging them to place their hands on window touchscreens if they wanted to do a good deed. Among the suggestions subsequently appearing on the window were 'make the person beside you laugh', 'pay for someone's coffee in line behind you' and 'say thank you to someone who served in the armed forces'. As Gap and Bombas raised awareness of the issue of homelessness, they united consumers in a common cause. By making a difference through the purchase of socks, consumers enjoyed a feel-good moment coupled with a sense of immediate gratification.

Season Neutral

When British brand Burberry announced its decision to take a 'season-neutral' approach to fashion, it broke away from the convention of designing separate autumn/winter and spring/summer collections. In future, each of Burberry's collections will include clothing for all seasons, making it relevant for retailers in the southern hemisphere, who usually lag a season behind. Not only will retailers around the globe be able to place orders at the same time; consumers will also be able to shop directly from the catwalks, disrupting the fashion-week norm of waiting four months before collections appear in stores.

Both Tom Ford and Paris-based collective Vetements have switched to season-neutral presentations and the implementation of a buy-it-off-the-catwalk plan. Vetements is aiming for shows in January and June rather than February/March and September/October, cleverly tapping into the pre-collection budgets of bigger retailers and potentially giving the garments a longer shelf life before markdown periods begin. The possibility of ordering clothes straight off the catwalk may make it difficult to lure consumers into boutiques before the sales start. The season-neutral paradigm offers clients a chance to buy a year-round wardrobe as soon as new collections are shown on the catwalk, heralding a major shake-up for the fashion industry and a move that may rock conventional retail to the core.

Sexy Sells

When fashion brands advertised intimate apparel on adult entertainment sites, some consumers raised concerns about ethics, while others just bought the lingerie straight off the site. Sex definitely sells, so when Diesel divulged plans to feature its 2016 advertising campaigns on Pornhub and Youporn, it seemed like a savvy move. Perhaps less provocatively, Diesel's ads will also be on dating apps Grindr and Tinder. Diesel models on Tinder will appear to be users, and the ads will pop up as users swipe through local profiles. Diesel follows hot on the heels of J.W.Anderson, which streamed its collection exclusively on Grindr last year. Not only do these platforms operate outside conventional retail channels; they have the potential to connect with consumers' everyday routines. The content that brands will produce for adult forums may reach consumers at times when the urge to show off their sex appeal is heightened, making products seem especially relevant in the heat of the moment. Combined with a 'buy' button, adult forums become as shoppable as Twitter (as shown by Burberry, which trialled Twitter's new 'buy' button during a fashion-week show). Like branded video series that include digital tags and links to online retail, adult sites may also make viewing and shopping a seamless fit.

Today, connected consumers expect brands to connect with them on all channels and in all spaces where they spend time – in virtual worlds and in physical surroundings. Brands rely increasingly on original content to make their messages more authentic and are more likely to encourage consumers to *participate* rather than shop. As impulse and emotion are harnessed in real time, brand loyalty becomes an authentic experience that transcends virtuality. ●

Photo Grégoire Vieille, courtesy of Louis Vuitton Malletier

It's easier for fashion brands to explore historical narratives through exhibitions than with retail operations; a good example is Louis Vuitton's Volez, Voguez, Voyagez, an exhibition held at the Grand Palais in Paris.

8 Ways to Diversify Retail

Stage Events

Always in the right place at the right time, Nike plans its ***pop-ups*** to coincide with major sports events worldwide.

Photo courtesy of Nike

In the lead-up to Super Bowl 50, The Mint in San Francisco hosted Nike+ The Opening experience, which allowed fans to test products in the location's Arena, explore the Lab, tour the Hall of Speed and, if lucky, meet famous athletes.

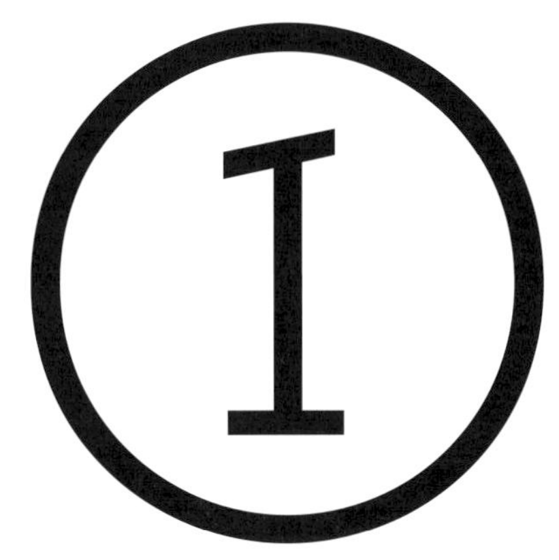

Nike and basketball: a slam-dunk and a glorious partnership embodied in the iconic Jordan brand. However, until 2017 it has to sit in the shadow of NBA kit sponsor Adidas, which dominates the court from the calf up by supplying every team uniform. Despite the German company's current advantage, Nike relies on its retail 'A' game to ensure that it's still heavily represented when it matters. After the success of the Pearl Pavilion last year (*Frame* 104, p. 207), the sportswear giant rolled up to America's two most beloved sporting events in 2016 with a new and improved event-related pop-up strategy.

Nike's bid for MVP in San Francisco and Toronto during Super Bowl 50 and All-Star Weekend, respectively, was pretty much the same. One: hit the host city hard and fast without neglecting other major cities – get NYC and LA in the loop as well. Two: give the fans what they want – meet and greets with the stars, classic sneaker showcases and exclusive access to new-release sneakers. Three: provide an innovative high-tech experience that puts fans in the shoes of their heroes, while generating word of mouth and clicks throughout the rest of the world. It's a potent cocktail of sport, product, technology and star power that has fans queuing up to get in. And perhaps most importantly for Nike, access is strictly member-only, allowing the brand to forge ever-stronger links with its customer base.

In San Francisco, home of Super Bowl 50, the success of another Nike initiative was visible: Run with Hart, the global running sensation in which US comedian Kevin Hart draws vast crowds of willing joggers to run 5 km with him. For gridiron fans, Run with Hart was transformed into running and training sessions that were graced by Nike athletes, who put the icing on the (presumably local) cake. In Toronto, the star of the show was the Jordan Standard, an immersive experience in which participants used body-tracking and ball-control technology to test their speed, control, agility and focus. As if that wasn't enough, there was even a barbershop on site. Now *that*'s sharp. — WG

nike.com

Get Closer

Hosting rather than serving clients, Ikea steps away from the confines of a store to facilitate ***social gatherings.***

Fully furnished and stocked with Ikea products, Kuchnia Spotkań provides Ikea customers with a venue for dinner parties and get-togethers.

Photo Karol Tomaszewski

What does it mean to be truly sustainable? Well, for global heavyweights like Ikea, sustainability is a concept worth pursuing. The retail brand has been criticized for its 'fast furniture' approach, but incorporating longevity and environmental consciousness into its furniture range suddenly appears to be the least of its problems.

At a recent Guardian Sustainable Business conference, Ikea's head of sustainability, Steve Howard, said he believes that the appetite of Western consumers for home furnishings has reached its peak: 'If we look on a global basis, in the West we have probably hit peak stuff. We talk about peak oil. I'd say we've hit peak red meat, peak sugar, peak stuff . . . peak home furnishings.'

So in the face of possible product obsolescence, what is Ikea doing? Moving beyond its colossal blue-walled retail outlets, Ikea is immersing its brand in a more intimate light, curating product and space to enhance the social and emotional experience.

In Warsaw, Poland, Ikea launched Kuchnia Spotkań ('kitchen encounters'), a fully furnished apartment where family and friends can host dinner parties and special get-togethers. Occupying a historical building at the centre of Warsaw, Kuchnia Spotkań encompasses an Ikea kitchen (fully stocked with tableware and utensils for cooking and eating, as well as garnishes and seasonings), a dining room and a children's playroom. Ikea's guests bring only ingredients for the meal they want to prepare and serve. It's a retail-inspired environment that speaks to 'heart over head'.

While material consumption might be approaching its limits, the appeal of living, feeling and sharing will never run out. It's obvious that today's brands are very much into sharing. Freed from the confines of product presentation, possibilities for retail become a little more limitless. — AB

kuchniaspotkan.pl

The first floor of Gentle Monster's second Seoul flagship, in Hongdae, hosts the Quantum Project, which tells a new story every 25 days. In February, the Dreamer's Hotel offered shoppers a space to take a break.

FRAME The digital magazine takes you inside the Dreamer's Hotel

The 26th evolution of the Quantum Project, Beating Beats, saw the space covered in orange fringes, tambourines and hand drums. Camouflaged dancers seemed to appear out of nowhere.

Photos courtesy of Gentle Monster

Shape Experiences

Marrying art with commerce, South Korean eyewear brand Gentle Monster engages clients with ***immersive in-store exhibitions.***

Retail has evolved from logo to brand image to storytelling to emotional experience. As the world shrinks and homogenizes, consumers want a 'pull culture' instead of the 'push culture' and hard sell of traditional advertising. Stores must be stories in 3D rather than simply retail spaces. Artist Tobias Rehberger (*Frame* 98, p. 115) crowded his cafés with dazzle graphics in room-size works. Appliance giant Electrolux craned its itinerant restaurant onto rooftops around the world. Now, four-year-old South Korean eyeglass company Gentle Monster also synthesizes art and commerce, temporary and permanent, in its shops.

The brand's name refers to the wish we all have, at some level, to try living someone else's life, a wish that becomes a hidden monster – curious and envious – lodged at the back of the mind. Aptly, the brand's fashion specs and sunglasses are diverse catwalk characters: sculptural frames, geometric frames, transparent frames with cobalt lenses. Equally theatrical is the design of its five Seoul flagship stores, which also serve as rotating exhibition venues: platforms and galleries for imaginative marketing and artist collaborations. In charge of visual directing and spatial design are Monster's in-house teams, which include art directors, fashion editors, fine artists, sculptors, scenographers, filmmakers, graphic designers and photographers. Instead of building a single costly store in the Hongdae area of Seoul, they divided the budget by 12 to create the Quantum Project: a dozen serial 'cultural' interiors, one for each month of the year. Subsequently, the 167-m^2 space morphed from a mirrored crystalline landscape to the experimental Dreamer's Hotel, open for 25 days, where visitors napped in hammocks. 'It is an emotional storytelling space,' says Quantum Project leader Dojin Choi. 'Dreamer's Hotel provided a glimpse of an experimental lifestyle and invited guests to become fully engaged and part of the experience.' Choi also points out that Gentle Monster wants customers to focus on *value*, not *product*.

Upstairs at the Hongdae flagship, shoppers find a variety of spaces, such as a marble room, a room ringed with old rocking chairs, and a garden of gravel and cacti. Another flagship, Bathhouse, was built in a derelict bathhouse. The Kitchen, a pop-up open for eight months, occupied an abandoned restaurant. The latter two excavated the original architectural details and synthesized them with a new creative concept. 'The goal is to give visitors a pulse-quickening experience,' says founder and creative director Hankook Kim. 'Although we can't rule out the commercial aspect entirely, we always think about consumers' emotions. We want to give them a chance to liberate themselves from daily life and jump into an entirely different world.' — SM

gentlemonster.com

Think Local

X Bank – W Hotel Amsterdam's retail outlet – offers a fresh, locally inspired take on the ***hotel giftshop.***

Branded T-shirts, cigars, teddy bears – a quick summary of what's in stock at your average hotel giftshop. And when the hotel is part of a worldwide chain, you can probably buy exactly the same items at the organization's hotels in Cape Town or London. X Bank, the retail outlet that caters to guests of W Hotel Amsterdam, is an exception. Suitable for no other location, the emporium features the *crème de la crème* of *Dutch* fashion, art and design. It's a shopping paradise that differentiates the identity of W Amsterdam from all other W Hotels. By focusing on the work of Dutch designers, X Bank creates a sense of place.

If you're wondering about the name, it's because the store is in an old bank just across the road from the W Hotel (ex-bank, get it?). X Bank now marks the spot for two floors and 700 m^2 of premium Dutch creativity. The ground floor is an art gallery that hosts lectures, talks and exhibitions, but we're going to focus on the first floor, a cutting-edge space that 'is set to shake up the hotel and retail industry', according to W Amsterdam's owner, Liran Wizman. It serves as a platform for 180 (predominately) Dutch designers – from young fashion talent like Barbara Langendijk to established names like Bas Kosters, from up-and-comers noticed by *Frame* – think Arnout Meijer and Rens – all the way up to Marcel Wanders, and from underground streetwear labels such as Daily Paper to global players like G-Star Raw.

The collection has been carefully curated by two insiders from the Dutch cultural scene: Mariette Hoitink, founder of Dutch fashion institute HTNK, and Gijs Stork, the man behind gallery Magazijn and other artistic ventures. They work alongside W Hotels to ensure that apart from being *the* go-to retail destination in town, X Bank promotes Dutch designers – and sells their products – on a national and international level. X Bank wants to support emerging talent, to help big brands get bigger and to be an ideal display window for premium labels – not to mention for W Amsterdam itself. The store adds a new edge to the old chestnut – 'exit through giftshop' – entirely fitting for a premium hotel that offers a 'holistic lifestyle experience'. — WG

xbank.amsterdam

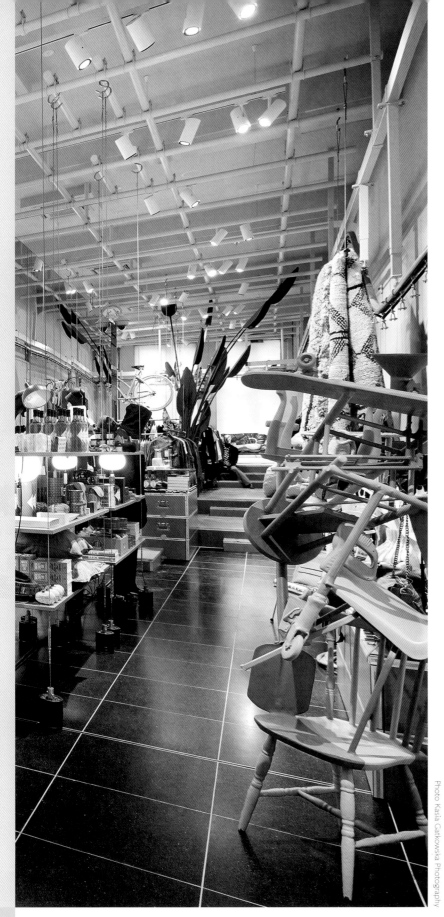

Photo Kasia Gatkowska Photography

Extending the W Hotel Amsterdam brand with a collection of home-grown products, X Bank is *the* place to go for Dutch fashion, art and design.

Once a year, the interior of the boutique-cum-gallery run by Beirut-based fashion foundation Starch is designed by a different studio.

See Elie Metni's system in action with the digital magazine

Photos Charbel Saade

Foster Talent

Offering young fashion designers the opportunity to 'take over' its boutique temporarily, Starch provides a ***platform*** for kick-starting creative careers.

For Starch, Elie Metni stacked 70 modular stools to create a temporary installation for displaying collections by Lebanese fashion designers; the configuration changes as customers buy clothing and stools and new collections are presented.

'I think store designs should get simpler as products become more complex,' says Elie Metni, whose super-simple shop interior for Beirut-based fashion foundation Starch is nearing its expiration date at the time of writing. Every year the nonprofit helps launch four to six Lebanese fashion designers by guiding them in the production of a collection, from conception through marketing. Meanwhile, Starch rotates their debut collections through its boutique-cum-gallery, the interior of which is realized each spring by a different studio.

The 2014-2015 interior featured a regular monolithic grid of ceiling and wall hooks and bespoke light fixtures, all of it – furniture, lighting and overall interior design – the work of local architects Ghaith&Jad (*Frame* 109, p. 068). This spring's shop will be the creation of Vladimir Kurumilian. Between the two, the 2015-2016 Starch Boutique was fashioned by Metni, a former Herzog & de Meuron staffer who is currently completing a degree in architecture at the University of Balamand. Beneath a large neon ceiling lamp – flat, square and suspended – is Metni's freestanding display unit, which is reflected blurrily in a painted copper wall that divides the room diagonally. Allowing for the presentation of garments on hangers and shelves, the modular installation is made from 70 identical beechwood Emma stools that are slotted together by means of metal connecting strips. Metni's purpose-made stools and their connectors provide his micro-architectural assemblage with structure and ornament. Visitors invited to buy clothing and stools as the months pass and various collections are shown gradually reduce the number of stools and alter the layout. Apparel by the next fashion designer whose pieces appear in the boutique is influenced, therefore, by a modified configuration comprising fewer stools.

As a fan of temporary retail spaces, Metni hopes they become more popular. He believes they are more agile in articulating a fresh aspect of a brand while also retaining its essential character. 'An indirect collaboration happens among all the disciplines that make and present the product together, giving the visitor a new experience,' he says, 'a new way to interact with both product and brand.' – SM

starchfoundation.org

A transparent life-size home built from laser-cut acrylic resin houses a selection of the smart products Target has on offer.

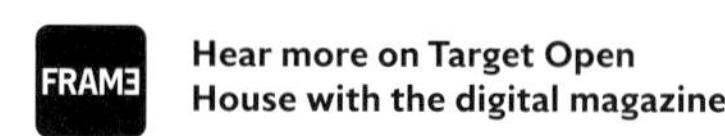

Hear more on Target Open House with the digital magazine

Encourage Interaction

Tapping into its knowledge of exhibition design to animate the retail scene, Local Projects invites Target shoppers to ***try before they buy.***

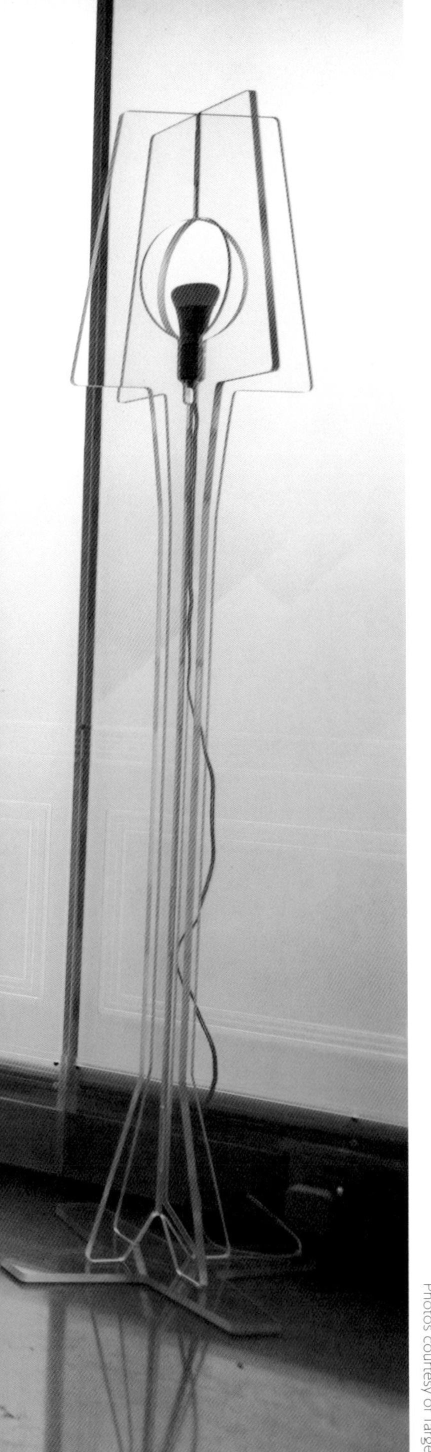

Photos courtesy of Target

6

The numbers projected are huge. The so-called Internet of Things – smart devices that connect us to networks of objects and information – is expected to swell into a $1.7-trillion market by 2020. Target, one of the biggest big-box retailers in North America, wanted a retail space that would let the company itself, and its customers, enter a store without getting lost. With that thought in mind, Target asked media-design firm Local Projects to translate its deep background in exhibition design – for clients like the 9/11 Memorial and Smithsonian Museum – into a commercial project.

Exploiting everything it knows about exhibition design, history and storytelling, Local Projects made a retail space in San Francisco that tells tales of the future. Target Open House is a 325-m² store where visitors learn about domestic smart products and how they can work in concert to resolve household problems, from leaky plumbing to sleepless infants and burglaries. 'Retailers can learn a lot from museums and vice versa,' says Nathan Adkisson, director of strategy at Local Projects. 'Retailers are waking up to the fact that their competitive advantage is the in-store experience. If they aren't offering one that's unique, they are left to compete with Amazon for the e-commerce market – and that's not a great place to be. Museums, on the other hand, have been thinking about experience for a long time. We operate at the intersection of these industries.'

At launch, 24 smart products were in-store that had previously been available only online – from the Nest smart thermostat to newcomers like Parrot's Mimo and Flic, a navigation/entertainment system that does everything but wash the car and the dishes, and the 94Fifty smart basketball – allowing shoppers to see, feel and hold the product before buying. Experience and education drive sales: in a transparent life-size home built from laser-cut acrylic resin, Local made store design a complexly interdisciplinary practice, involving not just physical design but interactive, media and technology design, not to mention motion graphics and production. The house contains transparent furniture and light fixtures, crown moulding and façades inspired by the city's Victorian homes, the Painted Ladies minus the paint, while one wall of each room, sheathed in light-absorbent projection film, serves as a responsive screen. As visitors select scenarios from touchscreen menus, motion detectors trigger greetings from 'personality-filled' products and each 'story', written in live code, spurs products into action.

A house with pellucid walls and partitions lets visitors see the invisible 'conversations' taking place among products. Adkisson explains that in the living room, when visitors select the Burglar! scenario, the house responds to an intruder. Sonos wireless speakers issue an alarm, Philips Hue LED lights flash red and Tripper sends an alert to the resident's phone.

The see-through property of acrylic was practical in another way. 'Early prototyping of the concept in stores showed that realistic furniture, even all white, distracts people from the products; they wanted to buy *that* crib or *that* bed,' says Adkisson. Acrylic distinguishes furnishings from products and reinforces the store's message – that the future lies in open platforms – giving Target Open House a double meaning.

Local has been asked by tech companies and, increasingly, by fashion houses to design retail spaces. 'In the future, everything from fashion and food to beverage and automotive will be considered "technology companies",' says Adkisson. It benefits both shopper and retailer when data is used to deliver an experience based on the interests of individual shoppers: what they have tried on and what they have bought. 'Shopping will become increasingly personalized, both online and off,' says Adkisson. 'The idea that you and I will walk into a store and have even remotely the same experience will be a thing of the past.' – SM

openhouse.target.com

Allison Crank's VR-based Reality Theatre enables customers to mix fantasy and commerce in the creation of their bespoke shopping spaces.

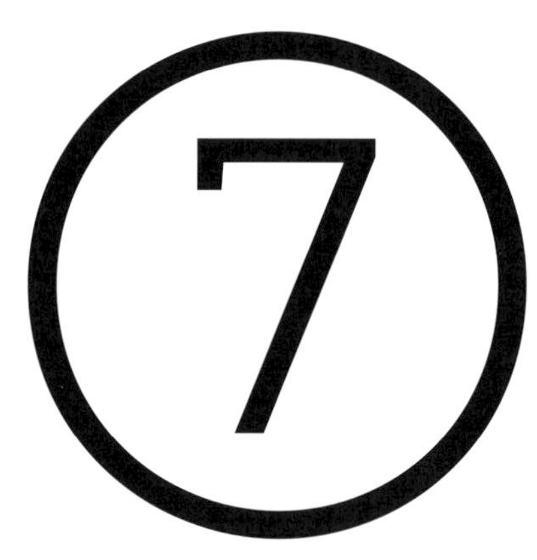

E-commerce is the fastest growing retail market in Europe. Full stop. It is an industry that coins terms almost daily – webrooming, showrooming, mCommerce – and, according to UK-based Centre for Retail Research, is currently growing at a steady annual rate of 18.4 per cent. Brick-and-mortar stores have been tracking this thriving organism since the dawn of the web. However, the future of retail will be most powerful if online and offline join forces. A combined approach has already proved successful for heavyweights JD.com, Inc. and Alibaba – two of China's top e-commerce companies – who are expanding their businesses beyond the internet by partnering with offline retailers, a decision analysts say demonstrates broader changes in the sector.

It's no secret that the multitude of gadgets on the market make for savvier shoppers. Originally, online outlets proffered sacred portals into the consumer's private world. Through exponential content saturation, visitors to such sites became more critical and the sites themselves more expensive. Desktop, mobile, tablet and – now appearing on the horizon – virtual-reality platforms all require expensive resources and constant care.

Financial issues are not the only reason that online businesses are feathering nests outside the digital jungle. Physical stores are a treasure trove of tactility. Consumers have been bandied through cycles of buying behaviour, most noticeably the sequence of online research and offline purchase – or vice versa. Retailers are responding. Last year Amazon opened its first 'physical extension of Amazon.com'. Retail's spatial design is becoming a hybridized beast of commerce. But the consumer is fickle. What happens when you throw in virtual reality?

Still experimental, VR is the latest ode to the coveted melange of physical and virtual stores. Although it's been reported that people get nauseous from a short spell behind the essential goggles – the first fully equipped pair will be commercially available this year – speculative VR retail projects are in the works. When British designer Allison Crank presented simulated shopping centre Reality Theatre, she described it as a 'playground for experiences'. Through a mix of fantasy and commerce, customers can create their own bespoke shopping spaces, edging closer to seemingly authentic experiences.

The future of retail may see a cacophony of online platforms, but a seismic shift back to physical stores underlines the human commitment to sensation. Although we're living more and more online, studies of consumer behaviour show that shopping by clicks is simply a complement to the richer adventure that comes from living – and buying – offline. — LM

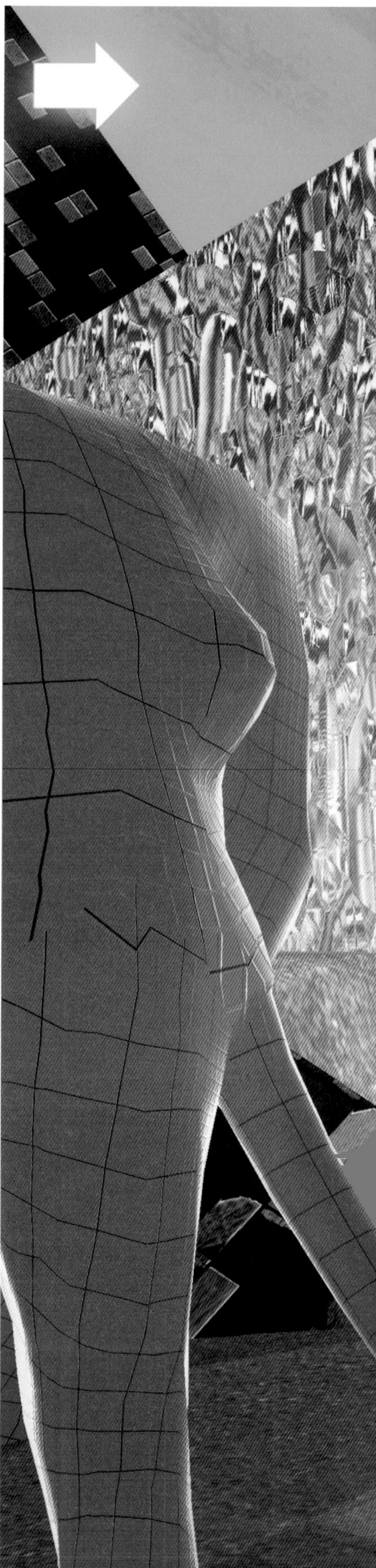

Go Phygital

A tool to enhance physical space, virtual reality holds promise for ***bespoke shopping environments***.

When O2 opened a concept store on Market Street in Manchester, it was with a view to transcending the mind-sets of conventional mobile-phone shops and opening O2's internal world of technology to involve the customer. Bridget Lea, O2's general manager of stores, describes traditional outlets as places 'people visit occasionally to make a purchase rather than visit frequently to learn and be inspired by the possibilities of technology'. Having recognized this behaviour, O2 moved beyond the fleeting retail models of their predecessors to take a long-term view of what mobile-phone ownership can be.

In a 2016 trend briefing in Australia, The Future Laboratory spoke of the gradual move away from heritage thinking: old ways of doing things that frame (and even limit) a brand's approach to retail design and services. Put forward as a replacement was 'legacy thinking', which is based on making every decision part of a company's long-term plans.

The interior of O2's new concept store draws customers closer to technology in a setting that represents both evolution and revolution. Developed and designed in partnership with Dalziel & Pow, it features interactive 'inspire zones', where customers can play with the very latest forms of technology, a broad array that embraces virtual reality, connected devices, mobile handsets and more.

O2 gurus are to deliver regular technology tutorials, which will start with rudimentary info on device connectivity and expand to include everything from getting fit with technology to keeping the kids safe online. Boosting dwell time are mobile charging stations and a lounge area that offers hot drinks. Best of all? The store doesn't discern between networks. 'Customers, whatever their network, are encouraged to connect with the store in the way that suits them,' says Simon Parkes of Dalziel & Pow.

Legacy thinking aims for retail immortality by taking the long view and giving consumers something that takes time to digest – and not simply consume. O2's substance-rich approach to retail design lifts the brand above the constraints of a highly interchangeable and disposable product offering, to a level that engages our enduring fascination for technology. – AB

o2.co.uk

Photo courtesy of Dalziel & Pow

Share Knowledge

In an environment dedicated to ***inspiration and education***, O2 encourages customers to explore the possibilities of technology.

Apart from retail, zones at O2's concept store are for relaxation and inspiration.

Show-Case

With the refurbishment of *Palazzo Fendi*, the luxury brand of the same name puts retail and hospitality under one roof, luring fashion fans and travellers in one fell swoop.

Words **Nicola Bozzi**

Photos courtesy of Fendi

Bas-reliefs subtly project from a travertine wall next to the red marble staircase that highlights Fendi's monumental boutique in Rome. The reliefs' subtly recessed arches reference the characteristic arches of the city's world-famous architecture.

Apart from Fendi fashions, a table by Massimiliano Locatelli is one of many design pieces that dress the shop floors.

Those using the boutique's VIP fitting rooms find custom lamps by Michael Anastassiades and art by Agostino Bonalumi.

Founded in Rome in 1925 as a family-run shop specializing in furs and leather goods, Fendi has evolved into a household name. In the 1960s, the Fendi heiresses – Paola, Anna, Franca, Carla and Alda – ushered the brand into a new era when they hired a young Karl Lagerfeld to head the company's fur and accessories department. At the turn of the millennium, *Sex and the City*'s Carrie Bradshaw turned the Fendi Baguette into a must-have coveted by women worldwide. More recently, Pietro Beccari's appointment as CEO has spun the company into a new cycle. His mission – to communicate Fendi's unique story – includes the opening of the brand's refurbished Palazzo Fendi complex.

The building is embracing its new role. Conceived as the embodiment of the complete Fendi experience, the substantial property now houses the brand's biggest flagship store to date, as well as an exclusive hotel and a private apartment. At the time of writing, the Zuma restaurant is set to join the ranks.

Shop

'We wanted to challenge the curiosity of the customer,' says Gwenael Nicolas of Tokyo-based Curiosity, who was tapped by Baccari to design the Palazzo Fendi flagship store. 'Fendi is going through interesting times. It's a very traditional, high-quality brand, but at the same time it makes surprising, fun and avant-garde designs. When you're confident, you can stretch both past and future. If you stay in the middle, you risk doing something boring.'

The French designer is somewhat of a Fendi-boutique veteran. This time around, the task was far more challenging. 'Rome is very dramatic by nature,' he says. 'We had to find a way to make the store stand out and get noticed.' The relationship between the boutique and the building embodies the tension between old and new for which the company strives. While no changes were made to the façade, the interior was freed of hindrances to encourage movement among its various areas. 'The first thing I thought when I saw the *palazzo* was that we needed to make it breathe.' The solution, he says, was to create a hole in the centre. 'We removed two staircases and two floors to open up the space.' In what is now the Italian brand's largest store, lighting and colour were almost as important as architecture in achieving Curiosity's objective. Apart from an elegant, cylindrical lift in glass and bronze, the most dramatic addition was a spectacular staircase in Rosso Lepanto marble. Nicolas discusses the stairs with enthusiasm. 'The red stone looks like blood. It's moving and captivating.'

Nicolas continues. 'It's about choreographing space, like a ballet. The store is a stage, but visitors have to discover it themselves.' Here, the choreography mixes a familiar Fendi-store atmosphere »

Finishing Touches

Displayed across the boutique, contemporary art and design pieces are mixed with iconic mid-century designs, all carefully selected over a three-year period. Some were custom-made, some bought, and others found or altered. Together they reflect the contrasts and dramatic beauty of Rome.

Behind the Scenes

On the second floor of Fendi's biggest flagship store to date, shoppers can see the brand's artisans at work. A glass wall separates retail areas from the fur atelier, exposing the fashion house's craftsmanship to the public.

with the venue's particular flavour. 'When you design a boutique for Fendi,' he says, 'everything needs to be somewhat subliminal. It's not just retail for retail's sake.' A prime example is a travertine wall next to the staircase, where bas-reliefs projecting from the surface feature subtly recessed arches that reference the characteristic arches of the city's architecture. These sculptural elements tie the visual narrative of the boutique to a wider, quintessentially Roman story. 'That's what's fun about branding. You create all these images – an abstract collage in a way – so that people who never entered the original building might "remember" it. You have to play with people's memory. You tell 5 per cent and leave 95 per cent open.'

Furniture also reflects the city's spirit. 'When you design a space you control everything; it's almost too perfect,' says Nicolas. 'You want to have furniture pieces that you *don't* control – things that break the balance and generate a different emotion.' The designer and Beccari agreed that this goal could be best achieved by reflecting Rome's innate penchant for sharp contrasts and dramatic beauty. Distinctive pieces were selected over a three-year period. Some were custom-made, some bought, and others found or altered. Each, however, needed its own story. In Nicolas's cryptic words: 'If you recognize something, then something's wrong.' Complementing the hand-picked pieces of furniture are others from Fendi's Casa collection.

Another idea was to have the influence of the city push the envelope – to be more daring than they would have been in a city like Milan, where luxury means something quite different. Besides the long list of one-off objects, dotted throughout the boutique are works of art and design, from Agostino Bonalumi's extruded canvases to the Campana brothers' Armchair of Thousand Eyes. According to Nicolas, the reflective sphere by Swiss artist Not Vital is particularly representative. 'This ball reflects the whole space. People who see it can take that memory with them. It twists perception and offers an element of surprise.'

> **“ That's what's fun about branding. You have to play with people's memory**

Speaking of surprises, Palazzo Fendi offers visitors an exclusive behind-the-scenes moment. Clothes are actually designed and made on site, giving the complex an air of craftsmanship. After passing through the retail space, visitors arrive at the fur room, where they can witness Fendi's artisans at work on the other side of a window. 'When I visited Palazzo Fendi four years ago, it was amazing to see how fur fashions are made for the first time,' says Nicolas, who was inspired by what he observed. Spikes used to make fur patterns cover an entire wall, and a 10-m-long tableau transforms no fewer than 50 unique fur patterns into a sculpture. 'Only when you go upstairs do you notice that it's made from Fendi fur samples. We tried to give the entire space an atelier atmosphere. That's something we could do only in Rome.'

Stay

Occupying the third floor above the boutique is Palazzo Privé, a private apartment for Fendi's VIP clients. Dimore Studio of Milan, an outfit previously commissioned by Fendi to come up with a collection for Design Miami 2014, was in charge of the interior. The duo behind Dimore – Emiliano Salci and Britt Moran – retained the original flooring and plasterwork but painted the walls turquoise to give the space a fresh modern look. Enhancing the salon's privileged ambience are contemporary furnishings by the likes of Bruno Mathsson, Axel Vervoordt, Marco Zanuso – not to mention Fendi itself – which offset classics such as a day bed by Giò Ponti in the entrance hall. Palazzo Privé's main room is divided in two by »

In the foyer of Palazzo Privé, a sculptural brass-and-glass chandelier contrasts with the classic features of the original architecture.

see-through metal shelving that features coloured-glass detailing. A large dressing room makes the accommodation suitable for private fitting parties.

Sleep

Although Palazzo Privé is available only to Fendi invitees, suites on the floor above can be booked by (affluent) members of the public. Marco Costanzi, the man responsible for Fendi's showroom in Rome, also designed the hotel, which comprises seven rooms and the accompanying communal lounge areas. His job, too, was to successfully blend past and present. In harmony with Curiosity's stairway are a reception desk in the lobby and showers in the hotel rooms, where the use of marble refers to Rome's rich architectural legacy. The colours chosen by Costanzi for the marble he used – white, green and dark brown – are similar to those found in the city's Pantheon, but sharply cut edges produce an up-to-date look and feel. The suites showcase Fendi Casa products alongside contemporary art and statement pieces, another good mix of classic lines and a modern aesthetic. ●

fendi.com

In the hotel suites are sofas and chairs from the Fendi Casa collection, as well as Marco Costanzi's custom-designed beds and lamps with leather shades.

The centrepiece of the hotel lobby is a marble reception desk in three variations and three colours of the stone.

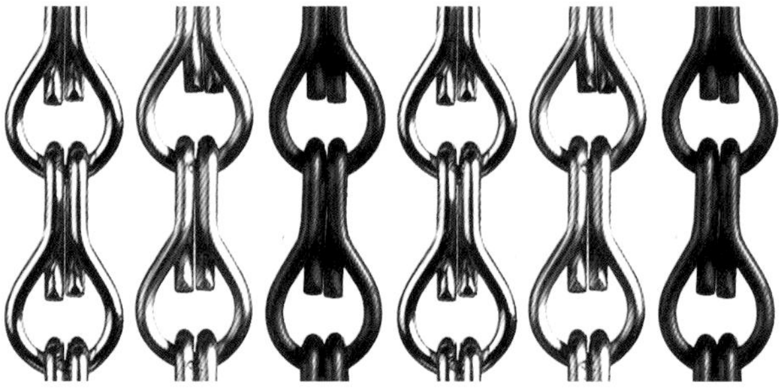

What's the Matter?

Design for a phygital world

Moving away from the *focus on craft and tradition*, Frame mounts a *debut exhibition* in Milan that showcases the *effects of digital technologies on contemporary design*.

Photo Zeitguised

i

'It's a mix of subjects we've discussed in the magazine from several different perspectives,' says Robert Thiemann, editor in chief of *Frame* magazine and director of Frame Publishers. Thiemann is explaining why the subtitle of *Frame*'s premier exhibition in Milan – What's the Matter? – is 'design for a phygital world'. The term 'phygital' has been stirring up the design scene for a while now. 'In our industry,' he says, 'you see a constantly increasing degree of cross-pollination between digital services and physical objects, and the impact on product and spatial design is significant. Take retail, for example: you can buy products online and pick them up in a physical shop, or buy items online with a tablet or mobile phone while you're in a real store. Virtual fitting rooms allow customers to select an outfit while browsing a digital environment and try it on instantly. Such developments demonstrate the growth of interaction between digital and physical. This is just the beginning. Phygital phenomena will evolve rapidly and affect even more industries, making the step from gimmicky objects to very functional designs an inevitable part of tomorrow.

'People seem to have regained their **faith in the future**, thus creating an atmosphere that is open to more experimentation in design.' Thiemann cites the end of the 2008 financial crisis as a reason for new-found optimism among creatives. 'We're experiencing a big shift from early-millennial concepts that were characterized by a longing for the past, as illustrated by the hipster movement and its focus on things real, authentic and local. Cafés with brick walls, second-hand furniture, cactus plants and lumberjacks with beards were everywhere you looked. Interiors evoked a sense of craftsmanship and tradition.' The lifestyle he describes seeped into product design as well, where it surfaced in the form of recycled and natural materials.

The counterpart of 'back to nature', says Thiemann, was 'an **interest in the artificial**, in everything associated with the digital: think display screens and pixels. Slick, superficial and available worldwide, but lacking tactility. Now, an emerging group is concentrating on a combination of both directions. Born digital, they refuse to recognize the immutable nature of solid substances. Instead, they try – often with digital resources – to breathe life into physical materials and, ultimately, to have them dissolve, disintegrate or liquidize. They're looking for ways to embed information-sharing and entertainment – mainly confined to technical gadgets at the moment – into our immediate surroundings without the use of mobile devices and computers.' He's depicting a future in which physical and digital become so tightly intertwined that it's difficult to distinguish one from the other. An era with no need for extra media-bearing devices but for technology that seamlessly, perhaps invisibly, makes information and entertainment an **integrated part of daily life**. Imagine a mirror that responds to the person gazing into it – or a sweater made to match your unique personality. Picture the flat screen of a tablet that becomes a three-dimensional light sculpture, or a fabric with a pattern flowing free as water. Everything around us will be phygital. ●

Born digital, emerging designers refuse to recognize the immutable nature of solid substances

Italian architect Ferruccio Laviani turns La Posteria into an immersive environment for What's the Matter? – a Milan Design Week exhibition presented by *Frame* magazine.

Reality **Check**

Commissioned by *Frame* to design the magazine's *What's the Matter?* exhibition, *Ferruccio Laviani* conjures an immersive spatial experience that supports the show's *phygital* theme.

Words **Floor Kuitert** Portrait **Antonio Campanella**

Renowned for his retail interiors and product designs, Milan-based architect Ferruccio Laviani comes up with the design of *Frame*'s first exhibition to appear at Milan Design Week. Transforming La Posteria in the city's Brera district into an immersive environment, the Italian creates a spatial platform for the phygital projects on display, which range from fashion and furniture to art and animation. In discussing the show, Laviani reveals his expectations for digital technologies in the world of physical design and explains how he turned the exhibition's theme into a spatial concept.

The digital world is influencing our physical surroundings to an increasing degree. How do you think this development will affect design? FERRUCCIO LAVIANI: I'm from a generation that has experienced the shift from analogue to digital. So the digital is becoming a part of my life, but at the same time I'm firmly connected to a more physical way of working. It's the interaction between both worlds that I find most interesting.

I'm quite sure that in the future we will be able to produce objects in an industrial way using 3D printing. That's got to be faster, more economical and probably more ecological. Nanotechnologies are also very promising. And all kinds of fabrics and textiles are emerging on the design scene that would have been impossible without digital technologies. I also believe virtual reality will have a big impact. Digital augmentation offers the possibility to travel to spaces where we've never been and don't have the opportunity to visit. It might be a different type of experience, but it *is* an experience. On the other hand, if you build an exhibition for a brand, visitors want to touch things, even today. Yes, you can use digital technologies as an extra layer that will help people understand the philosophy or the meaning of a design, but certain things require a physical presence.

Therefore, I don't believe it will be just about digital in the future. It is part of our job to find the right balance.

What role do digital technologies play in your work? Has their rapid rise influenced your approach to spatial projects? I don't refuse the digital, but I must say I only use it when I need it. Some of the guys at the office immediately feel the need to learn how to work with all the latest software releases. I'm not that type of guy. I think the computer era is coming of age. I already hear people complaining about being tired of answering emails every day. I think it's time for a different approach to the digital.

Of course, with the help of digital technology you can also do things that can't be done manually. In making the Good Vibrations cabinet for Fratelli Boffi, I translated a 3D computer file into a physical object by carving wood with »

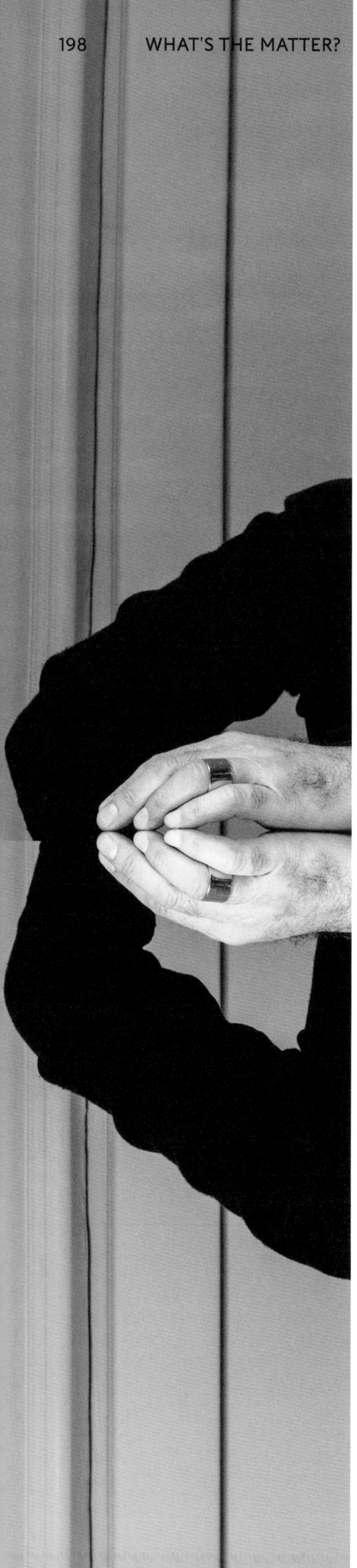

a CNC machine. The cabinet looks like a digitally distorted object. Its shape was greatly informed by the visual aesthetics of the digital.

Personally, I don't think all these new technologies can necessarily help me come up with a creative idea. Five or six years ago, everyone used the same modulation systems, and the outcomes were more or less the same visually. I'm not interested in that. But the fact that you can visualize a 3D environment in advance can help you to verify whether something works or not. At a glance, you get an idea of the sensation a space will evoke and how the proportions will feel to the users of that space. That's very important to the exhibition designer. But first *you* have to decide what you want people to feel in the space you design.

How does your exhibition design encapsulate *Frame*'s phygital theme within a spatial experience? As a start, I used an existing architectural element – the floor – and adapted it to suit the concept. I scanned and digitized the original pattern and reproduced it on every existing surface, much like a 3D rendering. Visitors notice a slight sense of disorientation, as if they're passing from real to unreal, yet in a tangible way. I selected a special adhesive film made by Exposize and applied it everywhere. The fantastic, rather unreal space we achieved has a somewhat psychedelic atmosphere that relies in part on optical illusions.

Like virtuality, reflective surfaces add extra layers to reality. How did you play with this notion in your design? The concept of distortion was my point of departure. The use of mirrored surfaces, as seen in the different display platforms, underscores the presence of the objects on show while also abstracting those objects and bringing about an element of confusion. Projections appearing at different heights throughout the space strengthen the impact. Moving images piled up on one another and superimposed on the patterned floor make for a metaphysical mashup of graphical layers. I want people to walk in and be surprised.

The location has a traditional Italian ambience, quite unlike the exhibition, with its forward-looking theme. How did you deal with the apparent contradiction between the two? The space has many beautiful architectural elements – details that can be invasive, nevertheless, and that compete with the type of exhibition we had in mind. I tried to take advantage of the location and to realize my plans without feeling restricted by the historical aesthetic. I did not want to fall into a category of the 'picturesque'. I wanted to create a whole new environment, an experience.

When designing a temporary exhibition, do you think about its online shareability? Social media are becoming more and more important to the communication of a project. But the high speed of such communication also makes it much easier to forget about news items quickly. A project might be mentioned by 300 bloggers on the first day it is released, but two days later it's already in the footers of these websites. Yes, you can reach people that you wouldn't be able to reach otherwise, but you have to do it in a smart way if you want them to remember. I would say social media are useful, but not fundamental.

What *is* important if you want people to remember your spatial designs? It's all about making environments that remind them of the fact that they are – in a way – inside the brand. Communicating brand identity should be about delivering a message that's easy for visitors to understand. Commercial exhibition environments should be brand experiences. It's absolutely critical during Milan Design Week, which is the most important design fair of the year. What you present here, and the way you present it, can remain in visitors' minds for a year – think of it as a souvenir. We designers have to meet people's expectations at all times. What we do and show in Milan makes us responsible for the communication of a brand for an entire year. It's nice, but very tough too. ●

laviani.com

Ferruccio Laviani

LOCATION Milan
CURRENT POSITION Director of Studio Laviani and art director of Kartell
(**PREVIOUS**) **CLIENTS** Foscarini, Dada-Molteni, Emmemobili, La Rinascente, Cassina, Flos, Dolce&Gabbana, Laufen, Piombo, Moroso, Emmemobili, Unopiù and more
LATEST PROJECTS Interior identity of Pasticceria Cova's worldwide chain of cafés and restaurants; and the interior design of the Kartell Museum, located within the company's headquarters on the outskirts of Milan (Laviani developed the original concept for the museum in 1999)

The Digital Virtuosity 2.0 by Bastiaan de Nennie

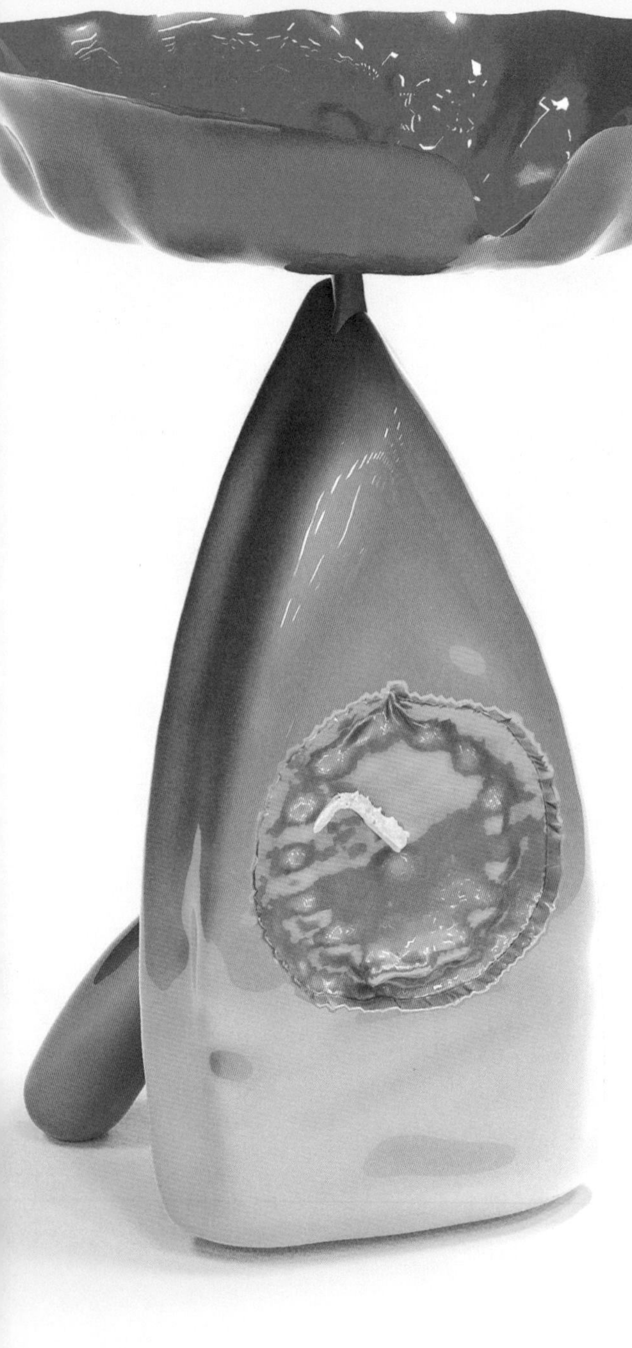

Dutch designer Bastiaan de Nennie's interpretation of Material Futures, the theme of *Frame* 107, splashed a captivating series of vibrant images across the issue's cover and contents. Hyperreal iterations of chairs made from parts of demolished cars formed the basis of his surreal scenes. Analogue components fused into never-before-seen objects that, after a bout in the digital realm, were deconstructed and reassembled. The finishing touch? A skin of shocking hues and unexpected textures. De Nennie hinted at his ambitions for the dreamlike visuals while talking to our interviewer: 'Even though the objects in my images and the materials they suggest exist only on the computer screen before being printed, I envision them finding their way into our off-screen world as well. In the words of Picasso: "Everything you can imagine is real".' De Nennie's fascinating images come full circle at the What's the Matter? exhibition in Milan, where his digital abstractions reclaim their physical state.

bastiaandenennie.com

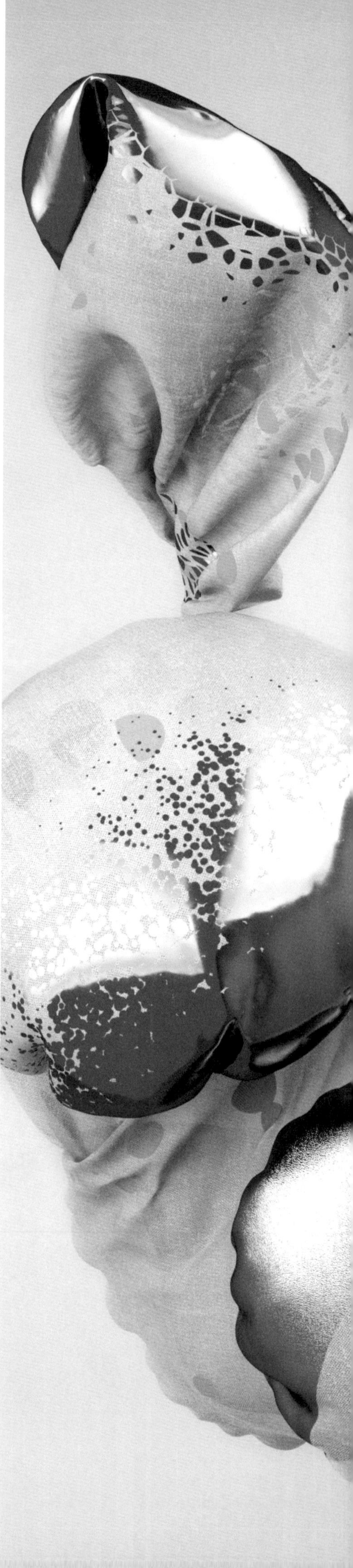

Bastiaan de Nennie, who converts tangible elements into whimsical objects with virtual means, returns the manipulated forms to their material state in Milan.

Geist.xyz
by Zeitguised

A collective of artists, designers and technologists, Berlin-based Zeitguised takes an interdisciplinary approach to concept generation and realizes projects with a dash of whimsy. The studio tackles art and design projects from all angles, including musical orchestration, creative direction and production. In the digitally produced fashion film *Geist.xyz*, fabric-sheathed objects spring to life as tactile textiles gyrate to funky beats, with no visible human input. A potpourri of morphing patterns, slithering surfaces, bobbing blobs and twisting forms: all aspects of the scene are affected, leaving only supernatural forces to blame – a poltergeist perhaps? – for the unexplained activity. A string of similar scenes are altered by means of an algorithm that remixes the behaviour of the materials all the way down to colour placement and patterns. Zeitguised's quirky world is complemented by a mystical layering of oscillating sounds by Superimposed Void, which does its best to convince viewers that what they're seeing is more than simply a figment of the imagination.

zeitguised.com

In Zeitguised's fashion film, *Geist.xyz*, supernatural forces breathe life into fabric-sheathed objects that gyrate to funky beats.

ABCD and O Tables
by Kukka Studio

'A dialogue between materials' is what Rona Meyuchas-Koblenz set out to create with Spectra, a series of objects for Kukka Studio. Combining Prinz Optics' dichroic glass with reclaimed quartz from Caesarstone, the Israeli-British designer and Kukka Studio's founder made two side tables: ABCD and O. Both demonstrate the 'material symbiosis' that Meyuchas-Koblenz was looking for. Unlike the unwavering physicality of quartz, glass is subject to constant change, a contrast that gives her designs a sense of ethereality. 'The glass is transparent, reflective and refractive; the quartz is solid, timeless, absorbent and repellent,' says Meyuchas-Koblenz, whose tables appear to reveal the colour of light. 'The environment we live in is affected by a spectrum of different conditions. Dichroic glass allows me to express the conditions influenced by light and time – and to reference the ambiguous conversation between the physical and the digital.'

Meyuchas-Koblenz finds it important to be present in Milan, where she graduated and took her first professional steps. In her own words: 'During Salone del Mobile, the city transforms into *the* epicentre of design and the business around it.'

kukkastudio.co.uk

Meyuchas-Koblenz's ABCD and O tables for Kukka Studio combine reclaimed Caesarstone quartz with dichroic glass from Prinz Optics, which reflects, refracts and absorbs light.

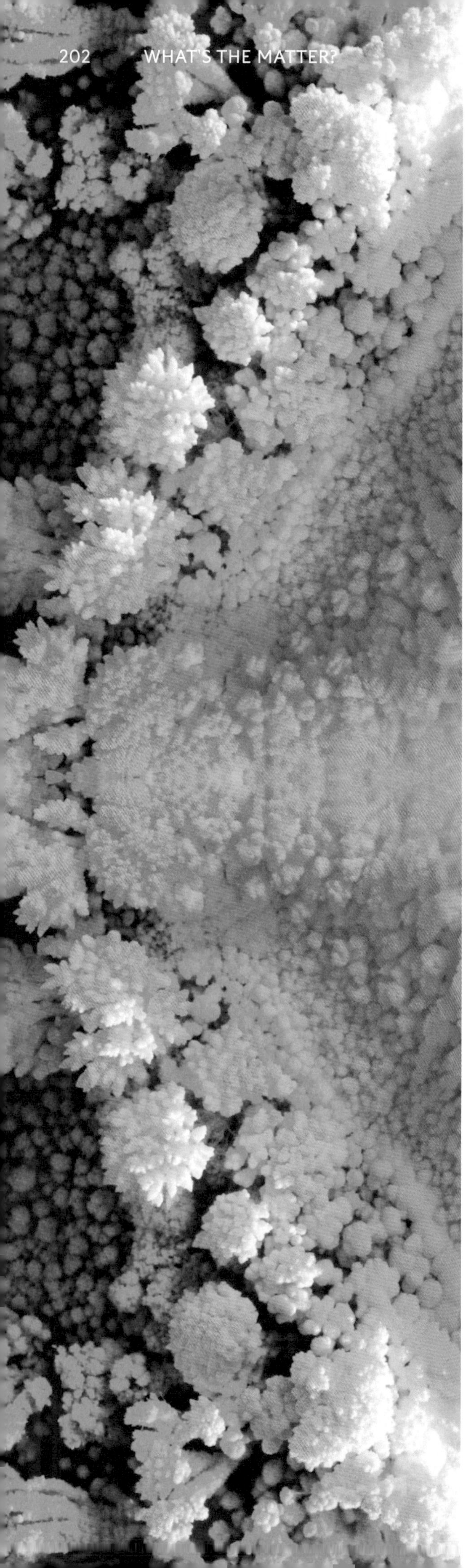

You Could Sunbathe in this Storm
by Alice Dunseath

Bewildering crystal formations sprout hairy appendages in Alice Dunseath's animated composition of geometric forms, psychedelic pastel swirls and sci-fi coral reefs. Stirring and awakening like the first signs of nature at the end of a cold winter, the scenes of *You Could Sunbathe in this Storm* are filled with familiar forms and alien hues alive in a world of fragmented motion. At her studio in London, Dunseath choreographs a cinematic dance that marries everyday materials, liquids, chemicals and crystals to music or recited poems. 'I use real-world footage and manipulate the imagery digitally,' she says, 'to make films that are, technically speaking, of and from the physical world but look otherworldly, like something you would never experience with your eyes alone.' After a jaunt through the digital realm, the originally analogue visuals are available for us to view as an enchanting sequence of moving pictures.
alicedunseath.com

***You Could Sunbathe in this Storm* transports viewers to a realm of enchantment, thanks to the psychedelic visuals that Alice Dunseath composed in her studio before achieving the desired result with the magic of digital imagery.**

Protection by Hyde Park

Filmmaker and musician Kamiel Rongen has a fascination with a land down under – under water, to be exact. Using the alias Hyde Park, the Dutchman makes subaquatic audiovisual landscapes that are alive with vivid colours and amorphous shapes. With a fishbowl as a movie studio, he manipulates the submerged scenery, devoid of gravity's strict rules, filling the vessel with a myriad of seductive apparitions. Liquids stretch, air bubbles bounce and dust clouds burst to Rongen's musical score, written to express the mood of whatever film he's making. Visitors entering *Frame*'s exhibition What's the Matter? find themselves engulfed in the volatile waters of *Protection* – without getting even the soles of their shoes wet.

hyde-park.nl

Audiovisual composition *Protection* exemplifies Hyde Park's clever treatment of scenery and music, the latter of which amplifies the state of antigravity in a fishbowl filled with water.

Photo Zi Yu

XI by Jim Chen-Hsiang Hu

Searching for a formula that might explain everything in our material universe, Taipei-born fashion designer Jim Chen-Hsiang Hu, a graduate of Central Saint Martins, turned to the energy of subatomic particles. He translated their grid-like forms into a unique weaving technique, effectively adding a third dimension to the once-planar process. 'The designs were initially meant to embody the invisible code of our physical world,' he says, referring to his work as 'an emergence' that blurs the barrier between different worlds. He believes his discovery 'parallels how phygital development bridges the physical world and the digital one'. Although Hu's 3D *weaving* represents a rapid dialogue between the digital and the artisanal, it is not to be confused with 3D *printing*. The intricate crisscrossing of his woven threads gives the fashions a sculptural appearance. Highlighting Hu's XI collection are swollen panels of laser-cut fabric used to make voluminous garments. One More Dimension, the outfit he founded in 2015, continues to develop 3D-woven fashions and to suggest possibilities for their physical application.

onemoredimension.com

The result of an intricate process of three-dimensional weaving, voluminous garments characterize Jim Chen-Hsiang Hu's XI collection: a rapid dialogue between the digital and the artisanal.

Anaglyph and Parabola
by Jordan Söderberg Mills

Jordan Söderberg Mills juggles the professions of designer, artist, architect and artisan. He's a *poly*disciplinary guy, with a varied background that includes studies in art history at University of Toronto's Trinity College; architecture at Diego Portales University in Santiago, Chile; a master's from Central Saint Martins, London; and a stint as a blacksmith in the foothills of the Andes. It all comes together in the crafting of material installations, objects and sculptures that defy physics. 'Digital artefacts can be deceptive – manipulated, tweaked and filtered. Physical objects have a truth and immediacy that emerge from materiality, purpose and craft. I set out to create experiential objects that bamboozle and play with truth and deception,' says Söderberg Mills. In pursuit of 'hacking' visual perception, he came up with Anaglyph and Parabola, whose lustrous surfaces reflect the physical realm in brilliant hues, turning ordinary into extraordinary. Backed by physics instead of computational programming, the mirrors act as optical filters, emanating wavelengths of colour also visible on a screen's grid of pixels.

soderbergmills.com

Photo Devin Lund and Sarah Keenlyside

In pursuit of 'hacking' visual perception, Jordan Söderberg Mills provides us with a filter for reality in the form of two colourful mirrors, Anaglyph and Parabola.

Skinterface by Ka Hei Suen, Charlotte Furet, Andre McQueen and George Wright

Until now, most virtuality-generated experiences have been delivered through audiovisual devices. Addressing only two of the body's senses, however, limits the ability of such gadgets to fully span tangible and intangible worlds. Believing skin to be the crucial interface between virtual and physical encounters, Royal College of Art students Charlotte Furet, Ka Hei Suen, Andre McQueen and George Wright combined their knowledge of industrial design, footwear design and engineering science, respectively, in a 'skinsuit' whose sensors 'convert virtual interaction into physical feeling'. Wearers perceive a range of sensations that originate from a digital source yet immerse them completely in the real world. In addition to the experience of transition, the London collective – now dubbed Sensory Architects – envisages Skinterface being used to facilitate interaction with virtual objects or people in fields such as entertainment, communication, virtual prototyping and more.
skinterface.co.uk

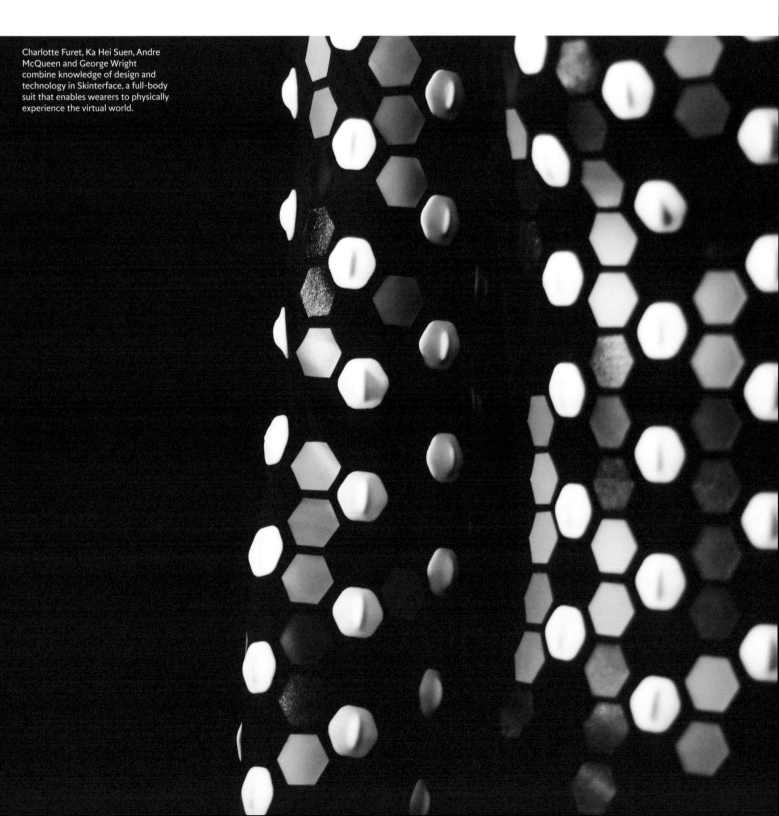

Charlotte Furet, Ka Hei Suen, Andre McQueen and George Wright combine knowledge of design and technology in Skinterface, a full-body suit that enables wearers to physically experience the virtual world.

Signature by Colors And The Kids

Berlin-based Colors And The Kids (CATK) doesn't like to feel limited, so the digital world's lack of restrictions – gravity, dimensions, costs – is the studio's ultimate boundary-free territory for creativity. Since joining forces in 2008, CATK's three founders dabble in art, music, design and anything that sets their imaginations in motion. CATK sees the digital domain as a playground for envisioning a scenario while ignoring real-life conditions – a space with an endless potential for enriching our physical surroundings. Symbolizing the studio's mind-set is *Signature*, a compelling animation of swivelling curlicues, psychedelic patterns and tactile textures. According to its designers, the video doesn't cover up the fact that they used a 3D program. What's more, *Signature*'s indeterminate 'purpose' might spark ideas for what it could become in the physical world.
catk.de

Realized without real-world restrictions, *Signature* is Colors And The Kids' digital formulation of an intriguingly tactile environment.

Dandelion Mirror by Scottie Chih-Chieh Huang

With a diverse background that includes several degrees in architecture and a position as industrial-design professor at Taiwan's Chung Hua University, artist slash designer Scottie Chih-Chieh Huang applies his knowledge to the development of interactive technologies for use in spatial settings. Along with his affinity for nature, Huang has a strong interest in human qualities such as consciousness and emotion, which are an important part of his work. Sensors embedded in his Dandelion Mirror respond to users by measuring their facial characteristics and expressions. The object's triptych of panels relies on a complex fractal and recursive algorithm to 'mix a user's self-portrait with emotion on a half-reflective mirror, triggering virtual dynamic patterns to form an alternative, functional aesthetic'. A stoic look reduces the number of dandelion seeds, leaving a bare stem, whereas a smile multiplies the seeds until they become a full cluster. Huang hopes the unexpected phygital encounter will remind viewers of the impact of a smile.

shkinetic.com

Photo Anatole Serexhe, courtesy of ZKM | Center for Art and Media Karlsruhe

Scottie Chih-Chieh Huang embedded sensors in his Dandelion Mirror, which reflects facial expressions as a dynamic – or dwindling – cluster of dandelion seeds.

Generative Scarves by Convivial Project

Comprising a team with interdisciplinary backgrounds, Convivial Project of London produces work that is an integration of art, design and technology. Cofounder Ann-Kristin Abel explains: 'The speed of human evolution is in arrears, owing to the pace at which our digital world is progressing, but we humans still need tangible experiences that stimulate the senses and objects that are tailored to our innate need to grasp concepts through physical interaction.' The studio's Generative Scarves collection is a prime example of her views. An algorithm-driven mobile app conceived by Convivial Project empowers wearers of the silk scarves to manipulate colours and patterns to their liking. 'As designers, we need to provide a smooth transition,' says cofounder Paul Ferragut, who sees this transition as a bridge between the digital and physical, a challenge to our perception that 'keeps us grounded and connected to the world we are familiar with'. An installation of displays and tablets at What's the Matter? invites visitors to personalize their own Generative Scarves.

convivialproject.com

An algorithm-driven mobile app empowers wearers of Convivial Project's Generative Scarves to manipulate colours and patterns to their liking.

Wonderfluoro
by Rachel Harding

Known for objects or spaces preceded by playful experiments with pattern, illusion, colour and material, Rachel Harding believes 'we are seeing the emergence of a post-internet aesthetic'. She talks about 'real, physical things that are inspired by the electrifying colours of the digital screen'. Utilitarian objects found in 70 per cent of public spaces, fluorescent lamps hadn't received much attention from designers before Harding got her hands on them. The ubiquitous bulbs benefit from her whimsical touch in a collaboration between her London studio and The Hospital Club. Using a diffraction film sandwiched between two sheets of glass in an aluminium casing, Harding came up with Wonderfluoro: a transparent tube that splits light into all the colours of the spectrum. She relied on RGB and CYMK colours for a collection that 'refracts light into its various digital components and electrifies the senses by creating 3D illusions in flat planes. Refraction glass adds a layer of unreality, editing the light and producing a Technicolor display.'
rachelharding.co.uk

Employing RGB and CMYK colours digitally, Rachel Harding made a fluorescent lamp that features spectrum glass and gushes rainbow-hued illumination.

Full Turn
by Benjamin Muzzin

According to Benjamin Muzzin, all animations are entitled to their personally tailored viewing devices. To accomplish this ambitious notion, the Swiss artist projects imagery onto bespoke displays that feature unexpected forms and materials. The ÉCAL graduate, with a bachelor's degree in Media & Interaction Design, pushes the technical limits of video-mapping by adding a twist to his cinematic presentations, sometimes literally. Atop a pedestal, Muzzin's graduation project, *Full Turn*, blurs the boundaries of digital and physical realms by rapidly spinning a pair of monitors set back to back. As they begin whirling, gradually morphing beams of light appear to lift off the flat screens and step into the third dimension. A play of light and shadow, the kinetic imagery allows observers to view Muzzin's 3D work from all perspectives.

benjaminmuzzin.ch

Photo ÉCAL/Benjamin Muzzin

A rapidly revolving pair of back-to-back screens describes *Full Turn*, Benjamin Muzzin's ÉCAL graduation project, which adds a third dimension to video.

Glow and Pillow + **Ball** by Lucy Hardcastle

RCA student Lucy Hardcastle, who has a knack for conceiving otherworldly images, plucked one from the screen and gave it a physical presence. She started with a digital rendering made with computer-modelling program Cinema 4D and ended with Pillow + Ball, a sculptural globe with a flocked-velour skin that rests atop a gleaming blown-glass cushion, which speaks to Hardcastle's background in textile design. In another work, Glow, nylon panels with a slippery appearance are paired with a translucent hoop. Hardcastle says her tactile pieces 'play with the tension between the physical and the digital'. Digital tools allow her to achieve 'a level of perfection' – photographic in nature – that's lacking when she makes a physical version of the object she has in mind. 'Visually, computer-modelling makes the impossible possible, while extending the possibilities of not just visual communication, but of the entire communication of design.' Visitors to What's the Matter? can probe Hardcastle's imagination while viewing her installation of once-immaterial objects.

lucyhardcastle.com

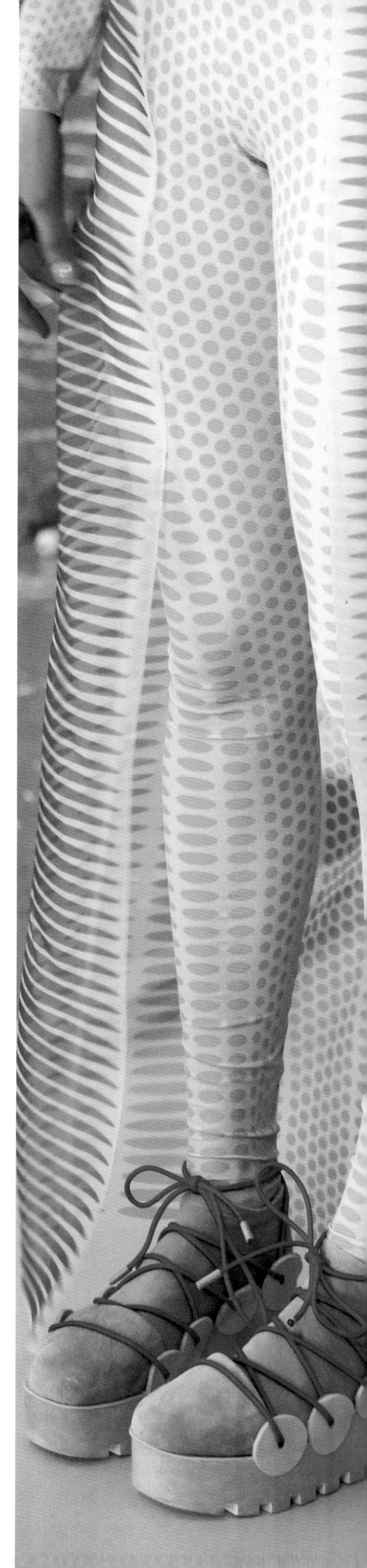

Generated by means of computer-modelling software, Lucy Hardcastle's otherworldly images materialize, becoming a spatial installation of once-immaterial objects.

Print in Motion by Anouk van de Sande

Dutch fashion and textile designer Anouk van de Sande speaks the cold hard truth: 'I notice the world losing grip on reality. People get lost in a grey area filled with their busy lives.' In an effort 'to excite and reactivate the human senses', the graduate of Design Academy Eindhoven's Man and Identity department turns her energy to something that nearly everyone interacts with on a daily basis. And no, it's not the omnipresent mobile phone that's seemingly attached to our fingers nowadays. 'Our digital lives are interesting and colourful, while our physical lives drown in a grey mass,' says Van de Sande, whose Print in Motion collection – a combination of materiality, motion, colour and shape – eliminates the static property of clothes. By layering translucent textiles with optical prints in vibrant hues, she conjures visually pulsating patterns featuring dots and stripes. When you wear the pieces and move around, she says, 'the clothes start to tell their own story'. The motifs 'look digital but are super analogue'.
anoukvandesande.nl

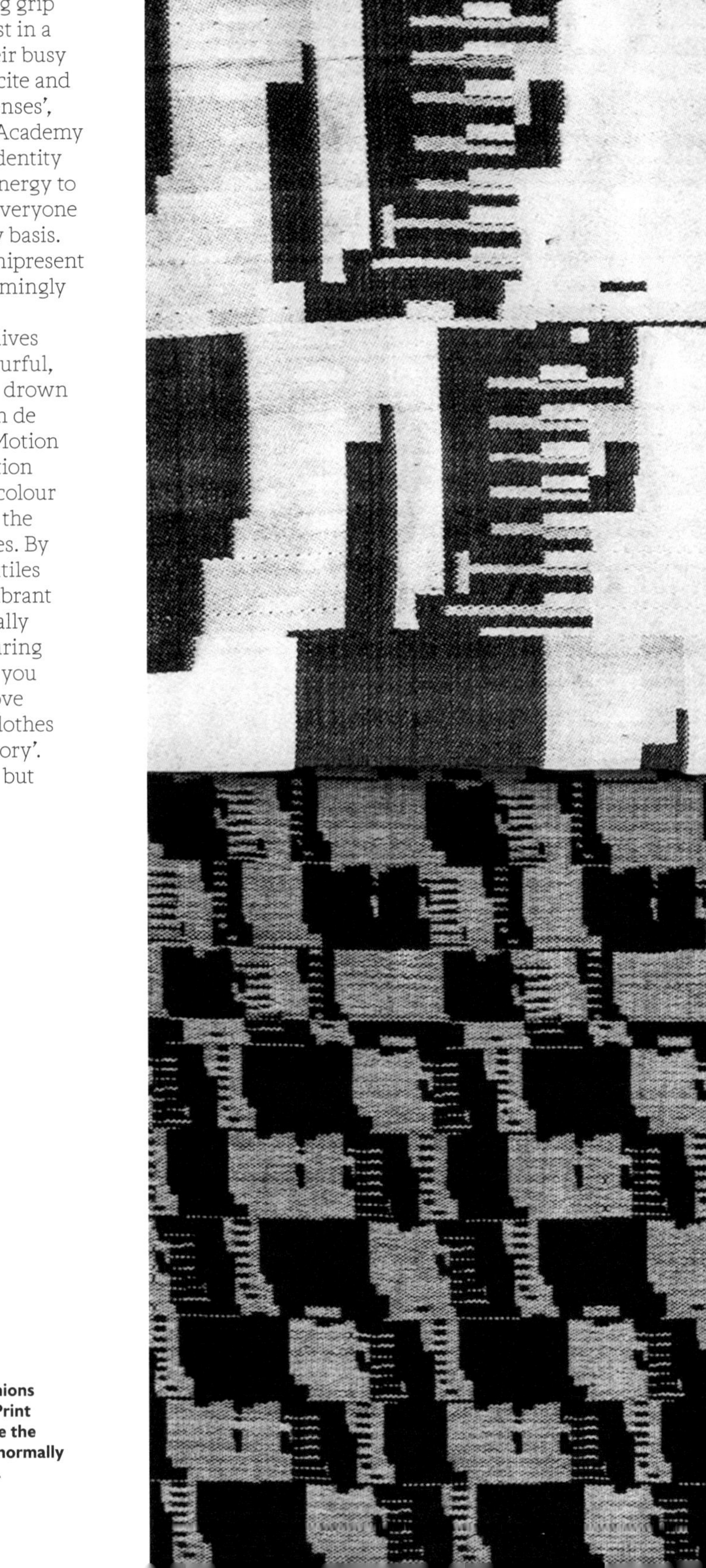

With a bit of movement, fashions from Anouk van de Sande's Print in Motion collection generate the kinds of optical illusions we normally associate with digital design.

Abstract_ by Julie Helles Eriksen, Bjørn Karmann and Kristine Boesen

With the 3D-printing bug spreading like an epidemic, the lucky few are becoming accustomed to tailoring an array of products to fit their lifestyles. Despite the increased accessibility of printers, however, producing wearable pieces of clothing is proving to be a challenge for even the most ambitious DIY enthusiast. To remedy the situation, three students attending Denmark's Design School Kolding – fashion designer Julie Helles Eriksen, interaction designer Bjørn Karmann and textile designer Kristine Boesen – developed Abstract_, which became their graduation project. The online tool facilitates the creation of made-to-measure garments through an interactive interface, but the trio took the concept a step further. During the interactive process, Abstract_ sizes up people with an interest in the tool and weaves their faces and stories into bespoke patterns. The Danish designers believe that technology aimed at the production of personally customized items holds an emotional value for the user, as well as the promise of a more sustainable relationship for all involved.
julieheleseriksen.com
bjoernkarmann.dk
cargocollective.com/kristineboesen

Abstract_ – an online tool developed by Julie Helles Eriksen, Bjørn Karmann and Kristine Boesen – can be used to personalize articles of clothing by weaving the faces and stories of customers into bespoke fabrics for the textiles used.

Global technology brand **Ricoh** – *Frame*'s primary partner for What's the Matter? – provides *digital tools* that bring the exhibition to life

HEADQUARTERS Tokyo
ESTABLISHED 1936
PRODUCT RANGE
Communication services, office-imaging equipment, production-print solutions, document-management systems, IT services
MARKET Over 190 countries worldwide
PRODUCTS USED IN WHAT'S THE MATTER?
Projectors, interactive whiteboards, Theta 360-degree camera

Created with Arjen Klerkx and Ape to Zebra, Ricoh's installation in Milan utilizes the brand's interactive whiteboards to video-map imagery onto physical objects.

Image Arjen Klerkx and Ape to Zebra

What's the Matter? explores a world in which physical and digital blur, a sphere that 'ties in perfectly with Ricoh's product and service offerings', says Oscar Mellegers of Ricoh Europe. This, the year of *Frame*'s debut exhibition, coincides with Ricoh's 80th anniversary, 'a significant milestone for a company in the fast-moving technology space'. Like *Frame* magazine, Ricoh has a strong legacy in print and photography: 'an undeniable bond with imagery'. For the exhibition in Milan, the brand joins *Frame* in uniting award-winning designers with industry-leading communication tools. It gives Ricoh the opportunity to 'illuminate the phygital future by showcasing our products in a different light, bringing to life our tagline – Imagine. Change. – which encapsulates how we're always moving forward with new thinking and new ways of improving lives'.

Integrated into the installations are Ricoh's projectors and interactive whiteboards. The latter enable physically separate users to work simultaneously on the same digital canvas. Built-in cameras allow visitors to communicate with one another, and their digital drawings and notes are video-mapped onto a physical object in front of them. Video-mapped objects for What's the Matter? mimic the surrounding floor tiles, thus connecting the digital process to the physical world. This type of interplay is central to Ricoh's core business: 'In tandem with the trend towards digitization, the continued evolution of the physical materials we use on a daily basis plays an equally formative role in the world.'

The *Frame* exhibition appealed to Ricoh for its 'different interpretations of matter, which – bolstered by technology – generate new perspectives and insights. As a technology partner, we aim to leverage this combination and make it accessible and real to the public.' The public he mentions extends beyond physical visitors; Theta, Ricoh's 360-degree camera, demonstrates its ability to capture an entire space in a single shot, extending the experience of the exhibition space beyond its physical presence in Milan.

Ricoh's key themes – integration, innovation and collaboration – are in the spotlight at What's the Matter? 'We're dedicated to giving a platform to artists and designers that enhances interaction between people and information through creative solutions. Milan Design Week is *the* global benchmark for design, and Ricoh is proud to be involved.'
ricoh-europe.com

Vescom explores the effects of a phygital world on the *wallcovering* selected for What's the Matter?

'The application of digital printing to a wall allows you to suggest something imaginary – a dream or a story,' says Christiane Müller, design director of Vescom, a Dutch developer and manufacturer of high-quality wallcoverings, upholstery textiles and curtain fabrics. 'You're imbuing an atmosphere with a sense of tangibility that involves both imagery and materiality. You can create structures that seem real, even though they're not. I see it as a new form of tactility and spatiality.' She's talking about a phenomenon that Vescom examines even further at the *Frame* exhibition, where a 5.5-m-long wall installation plays with the layering of textures and patterns. Vescom added Dennis Parren's CMYK lamp, which casts coloured shadows on the wall that seem to merge with the digitally printed pattern of Vescom's wallcovering. As they view the wall, visitors question where the light stops and the pattern begins. What is physical and what is insubstantial? 'They're experiencing a new reality,' says Müller.

'This exhibition provides us with a platform that can lead to the use of such walls in the future,' adds Nancy van de Pol, Vescom's marketing and communications manager. 'It's a physical result of the influence of digitization on wallcoverings.'

vescom.com

HEADQUARTERS Deurne, the Netherlands
ESTABLISHED 1971
PRODUCT RANGE Wallcoverings, upholstery textiles and curtain fabrics
MARKET Worldwide
PRODUCTS USED IN WHAT'S THE MATTER? Vescom's digitally printed wallcovering by Hanna Kohnen of Müller Van Tol and Dennis Parren's CMYK lamp

At the *Frame* exhibition, a purpose-designed installation features interaction between Vescom's printed wall covering and Dennis Parren's CMYK lamp.

Large-format prints from **Exposize** blur the lines between floor and walls at La Posteria

Collaboration with designers is key to the work of Exposize, a Dutch company that specializes in large-format print projects. 'To achieve the most breathtaking visuals, we need the creativity of the designer, which we translate to a spatial entity – using printed graphics as a tool – to produce a visual experience. In so doing, we position ourselves as a print partner, not just a supplier,' says Vincent van Herk, manager of the outfit's Eindhoven location.

For the *Frame* exhibition, open to visitors during Milan Design Week, Exposize assisted Italian architect Ferruccio Laviani and his team to push their concepts towards reality. After scanning high-res photos of the original floor tiles at the Brera venue, Exposize used the scans to digitally re-create the pattern on an adhesive film that's been applied 'everywhere'. The process makes the transition between floor and walls seem to disappear. 'Is there an extra dimension in this room that no one knew about? Yes there is, at least optically.' Van Herk is describing the disorientating effect that the repeat pattern has on the space. 'In addition, the textile wall film we used for What's the Matter? gives the scenography a tactile look and feel, adding another dimension.'

exposize.nl

HEADQUARTERS Amsterdam
ESTABLISHED 2001
PRODUCT RANGE Large-format printing projects
MARKET Worldwide
PRODUCTS USED IN WHAT'S THE MATTER? Textile wall film

Using a digital repeat pattern, Exposize multiplies an existing physical feature – floor tiles – of the location hosting What's the Matter?

Spanish brand **Atrezzo** is the exclusive supplier of *mannequins* for the *Frame* exhibition

'Physical meets digital,' says Alejandra Silva, who sees the encounter as an evolutionary step in the 'integration of today and tomorrow'. Silva is the commercial director of Atrezzo Mannequins. It's a brand that lets images speak louder than words; promotional clips, for instance, rely on process-related visuals – with a focus on handicraft – rather than on spoken narratives to tell the company's story. What's the Matter? gives Atrezzo the opportunity to explore how its distinctly *physical* merchandise performs in a *digitally* influenced sphere. Offerings from Atrezzo's collection not only wear the phygital fashions of Anouk van de Sande, Julie Helles Eriksen and Jim Hu, but also fill the contours of the Skinterface skinsuit.

Silva calls Atrezzo's participation in *Frame*'s exhibition for Milan Design Week a 'breakthrough'. 'In the 25 years of our existence, we've been quite cautious about who we work with and how we present our brand. This exhibition is exactly where we want to be. We try to be aware of what's happening around us – in the world of fashion, as well as in the areas of architecture, design and interiors. For us, the borders between these disciplines have always been nonexistent – we're constantly looking further afield and, of course, towards the future.'
atrezzobarcelona.com

HEADQUARTERS Barcelona
ESTABLISHED 1990
PRODUCT RANGE
Mannequins, torsos, props
MARKET Worldwide
PRODUCTS USED IN WHAT'S THE MATTER?
Mannequins: It Girl (female), Rocky (male); torso: MK – Columbia Action (female)

Physical figures from Atrezzo Mannequins display phygital fashions at What's the Matter? in Milan.

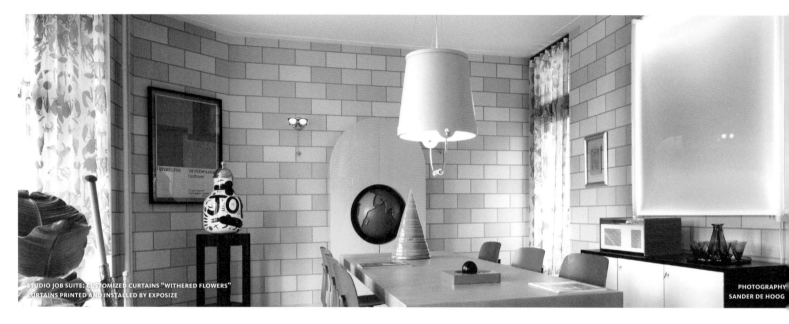

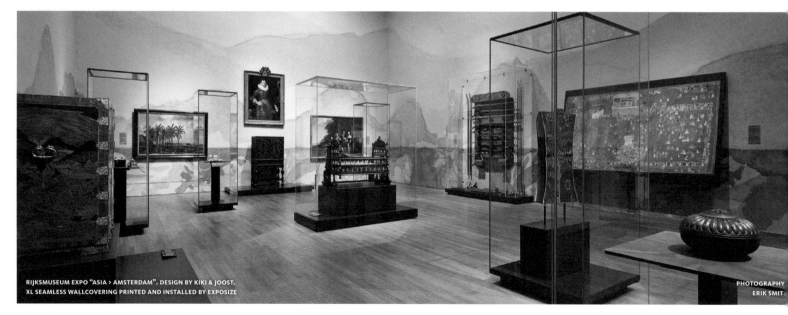

REPORTS Display

Hans Boodt considers the *future of retail*. Erco, Modular, Occhio and more have *display lighting* covered. Top mannequin brands get *back to reality*. Shelving-system manufacturers *opt to adapt*. Discover what's driving the business of design.

Photo courtesy of Window Mannequins

Hands *On*

As *Hans Boodt Mannequins* prepares to enter the premium market, owner *Marco Ouwerkerk* discusses the future of retail and how to adapt to it.

Words **Will Georgi**
Portraits **Anne Claire de Breij**

Hans Boodt

WEBSITE
hansboodtmannequins.com
HEADQUARTERS
Zwijndrecht, the Netherlands
ESTABLISHED 2001
EMPLOYEES 30
PRODUCT RANGE
High-quality mannequins
BESTSELLING PRODUCTS
Blend Collection
MARKET Worldwide
CORE MARKET
the Netherlands
DEDICATED SHOWROOMS
Rotterdam, the Netherlands; Milan, Italy; Melbourne, Australia; Paris, France; Tokyo and Kyoto, Japan. Others are in Germany, Scandinavia and Spain

Marco Ouwerkerk is a man who moves fast. Three weeks after he saw a vacancy for a commercial manager at Hans Boodt Mannequins in 2003, he was working there. Five years later, he was the owner. After firmly establishing Hans Boodt on the international stage, he's about to lead the company into a new era with the launch of its debut Premium Collection. That's not all he's got up his sleeve either, as the Premium Collection is accompanied by a quantum leap forward in terms of technology and service. On the day I visit Hans Boodt HQ, with its 1,850-m² showroom, painters and glaziers are rushing around, adding final touches to the star of the show, a new lab in which full-size prototypes will be 3D-printed on site. It's a veritable hive of activity, which is far removed from the atmosphere that prevailed when Ouwerkerk first joined the company.

'Coming from a retail background, the whole mannequin sector felt sleepy, old-fashioned,' Ouwerkerk reminisces. 'The first time I went to EuroShop, all our competitors were there as suppliers in black suits with nametags. We were fashion guys in casual clothing. Potential customers could see that we understood retail. They weren't interested in production; they wanted a partner who knew their world. It's the same here – how we present our goods shows that we can anticipate what's going to happen in the market.'

Our conversation leads seamlessly to the creation of Hans Boodt's Premium Collection, the company's first move into the high-end sector. 'It was born about five years ago, when we started exporting to new markets like France, Italy, Spain, USA and South America, where people felt that our collection was too Northern European, too bulky, and that it lacked finesse.'

Customer feedback was supported by internal analysis of the market shift to premium (which Ouwerkerk calls 'the magic word'). The far-reaching implications for the entire retail sector meant that Hans Boodt couldn't ignore these developments. 'Fifteen years ago, a store concept was built to last, so you'd buy an oak counter, an expensive floor and mannequins that would last a long time. Nowadays, people get bored by a concept within three to five years, so the counter is MDF, the floor is linoleum and mannequins are chosen to match current trends. As a result, the life cycle of a mannequin needs to adapt.'

The Premium Collection launches at this year's Milan Design Week (12-17 April), together with a collaboration between Hans Boodt and Marcel Wanders, who created two mannequins for the company. So what can we expect to see from premium mannequins? 'Two things: first, attitude and sizing, which is more or less irrelevant. If the mannequin distracts from the garment it's showing, it's not premium. In the »

An indisputable shift towards luxury in the retail market gave rise to the Hans Boodt Premium Collection.

casual line, the pose is a big part of the total window concept – it makes the garment look a bit better than it is. In our Premium Collection, the garment is the star of the show, and the mannequin plays a minor role. The second thing is the finish. Soft detailing, finesse and a high-end finish – whether it's chrome, gold or white gloss with three transparent layers – combine to achieve the premium feel.'

Hans Boodt's move into the premium sector is highlighted by its sponsorship of the Hyères Festival of Fashion and Photography (21-24 April), where the Dutch company joins Chanel, Swarovski and Chloé in supporting young creative talent. Equally exciting are the developments back home, where (as if you'd forgotten) there's the small matter of a new lab that will revolutionize the production process.

'Normally it takes about two months to make a prototype,' Ouwerkerk tells me. 'But two months is a lifetime in retail. In the lab, we can look at the product, make changes on the spot and complete the whole process in a week.'

It's impossible to talk about the future of retail without discussing sustainability. In this area, Hans Boodt is again ahead of the curve. 'All our mannequins are 100 per cent recyclable.

“ People get bored by a store concept within three to five years. The life cycle of a mannequin needs to adapt

We offer three free services if you want to get rid of your mannequins and recycle them back into the market as second-hand products. But all our customers are interested in recycling, because customization is a major priority for them, and that means new mannequins. However, as corporate responsibility becomes more important, I believe that taking care of sustainability will become a larger part of all businesses. And it won't be enough to offer a simple marketing trick; sustainability will have to be ingrained in the DNA of a company.'

For Hans Boodt, Ouwerkerk sees another fundamental change in terms of production. 'We are manufacturing mannequins on every continent where we sell them. It doesn't make any sense in terms of market demand or sustainability to ship a mannequin from Asia to the UK. It takes an extra four weeks and is really old-fashioned, especially in such a fast-moving world as retail.'

And retail is what it's all about for Ouwerkerk and Hans Boodt. 'It's my passion,' he says, 'especially the storytelling part. Without that, every store would look the same. What's our story? We know what's happening in the market and can make a mannequin that is a perfect match for your concept and customer.' I'm sold. ●

'All our customers are interested in recycling, because customization is a major priority for them, and that means new mannequins,' says Marco Ouwerkerk.

Brilliant *Beams*

Brands that deliver the best in *display lighting* opt for adaptability and subtlety.

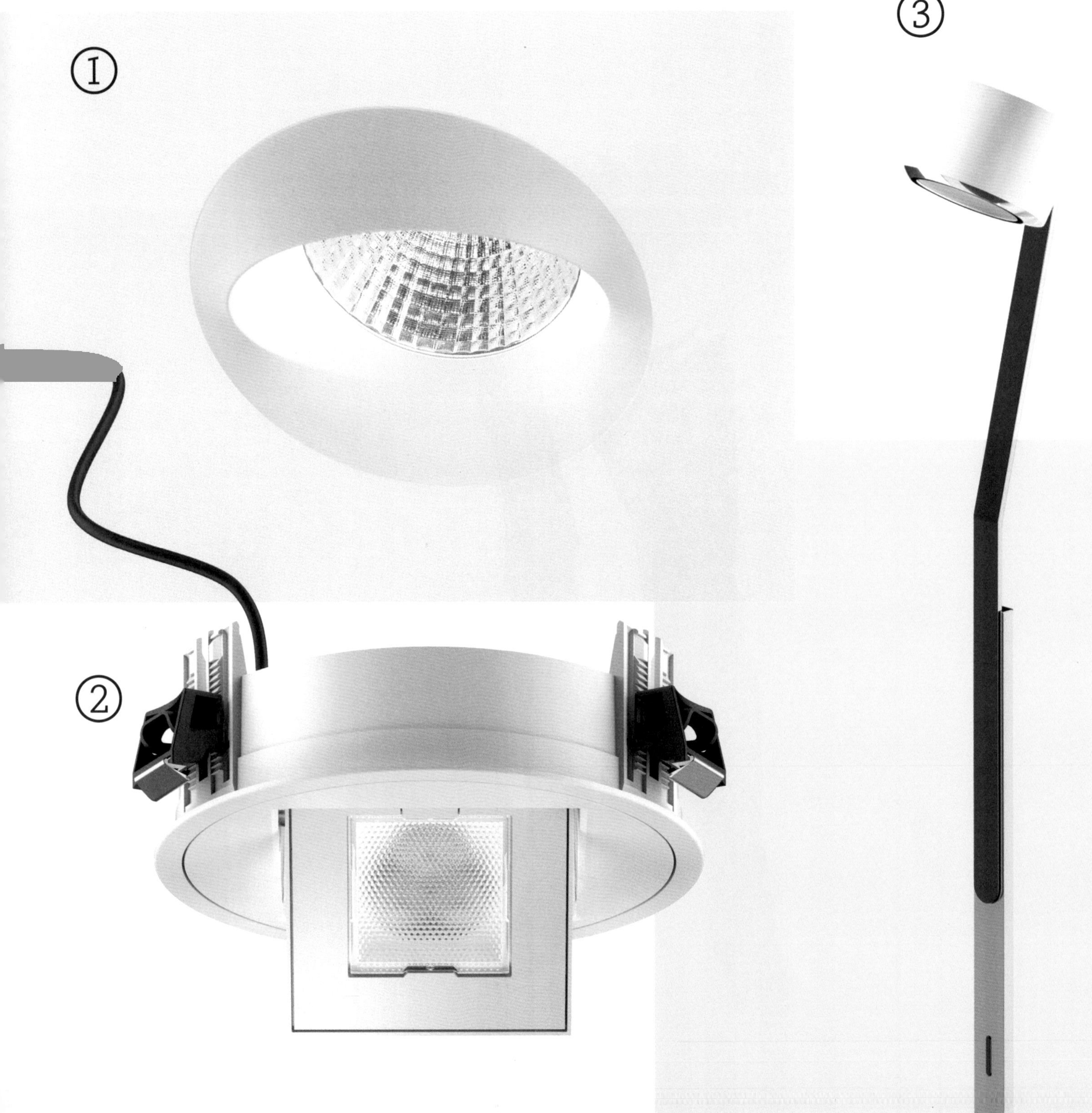

④

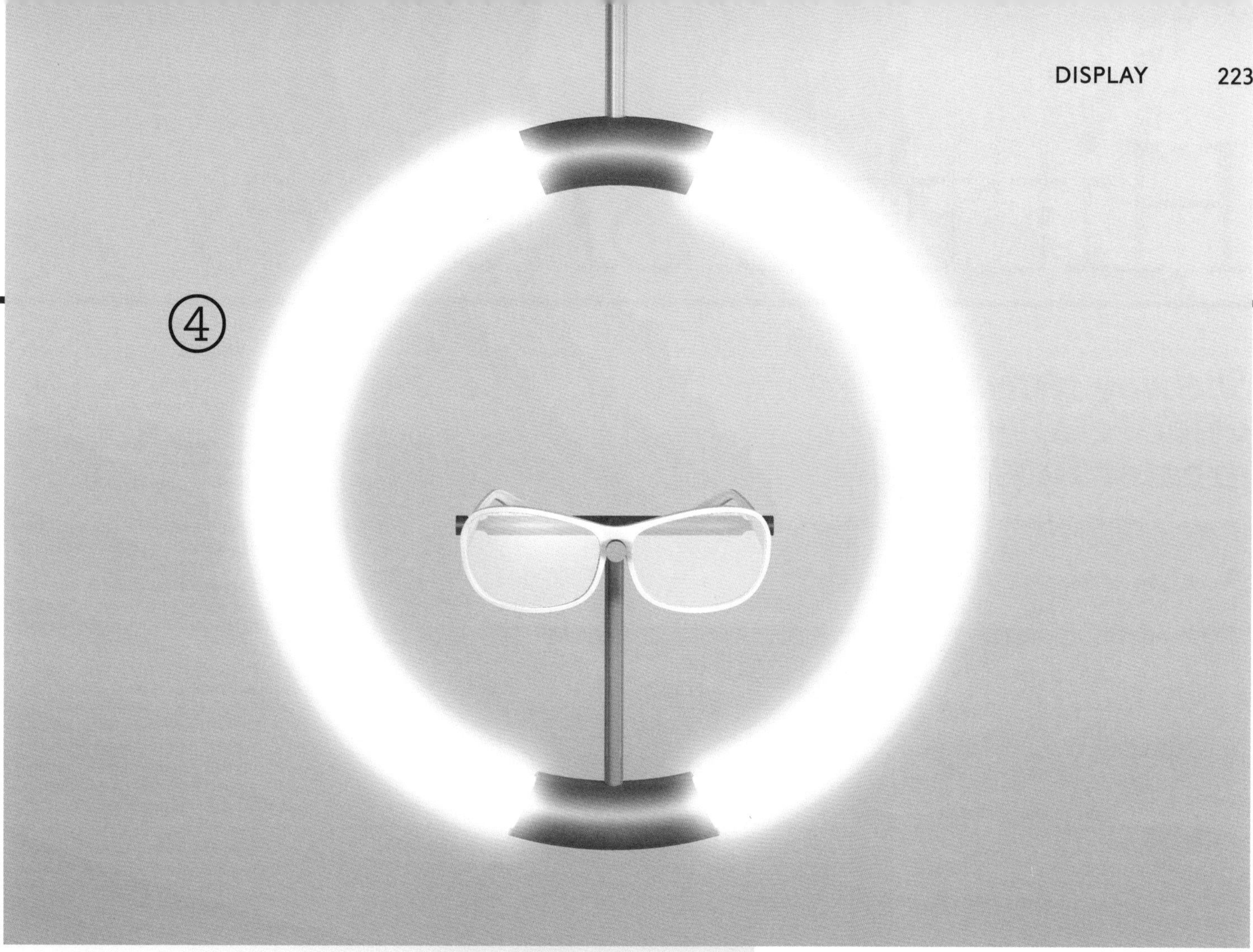

1 Wink by Modular Lighting Instruments gives integrated lighting personality plus. A design by Couvreur.Devos, Wink directs light through smooth contours that mimic the shape of an eyelid, producing a symmetrical and subtle downlight effect.

2 Tiltable and rotatable lenses make Erco's Cantax spotlights extremely agile. A shallow recess depth facilitates easy installation in areas with limited space for mounting.

3 Clean minimalist lines distinguish the Più spotlight system from Occhio, which features both recessed and surface-mounted fixtures. Employing the latest in LED technology, the extremely energy-saving Più lamps emit beams as pure as sunlight.

4 Designed with retailers in mind, Hudson and Broad's Lightstik system offers maximum impact at minimal cost. Both decorative and functional, the low-voltage lamps can be combined with the brand's matching shelving units.

5 Delta Light's Spy family is a collection of adjustable integrated and surface-mounted lamps that can be positioned at almost any angle, thanks to the brand's innovative Ex-centric Rotation System. A recessed LED light and removable inserts in white, black and gold guarantee a sleek and seamless appearance.

Hit the *Shelves*

Shelving systems **offer retail spaces greater flexibility.**

1 Hi-Macs acrylic stone is a solid, thermoformable natural material that can be used to make, among other things, undulating display units.

2 Vitra discreetly integrates LED lights and diverse multimedia into shop-fitting system Kimea P/L. Special current collectors provide low-voltage power for ceiling lights that illuminate merchandise.

3 Paxton's latest display system, Bamboo, gives retail spaces a graphic industrial aesthetic. Cleverly designed joints and tubing allow the imaginative modular system to be dismantled and reassembled repeatedly to incorporate accessories.

4 Prima's uncomplicated brochure display – the Prima Expo cabinet – features 15 hinged compartments, each of which opens to reveal extra storage space.

5 Vancouver studio Molo's Softblock modular system was designed to suit retail spaces of all sizes. The concertina-shaped structure stretches and contracts effortlessly to provide tactile shelving that doubles as acoustic insulation.

②

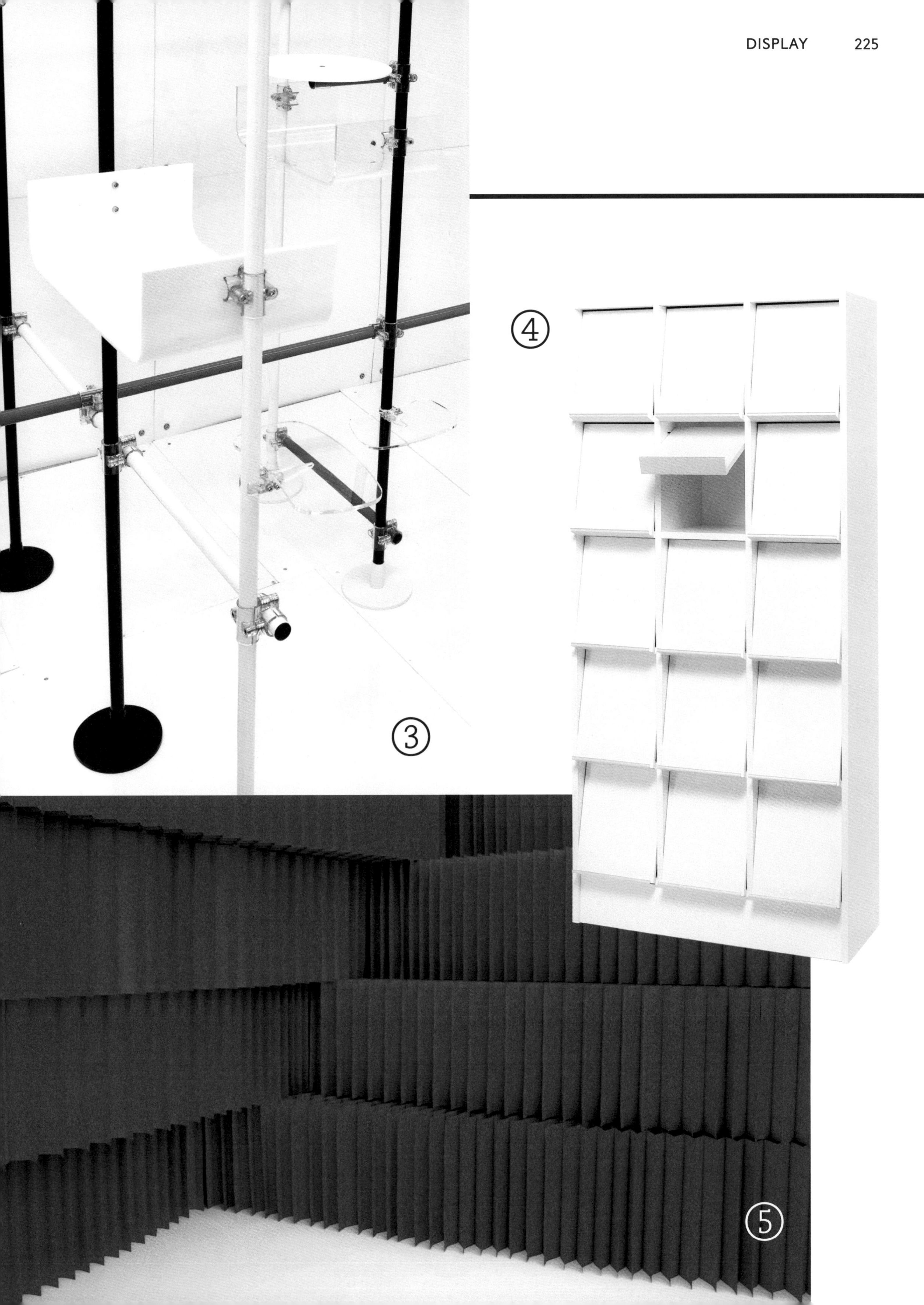
③
④
⑤

Body *Language*

Window Mannequin's Cameleon collection combines realism with abstraction, offering retailers a host of removable faces, eyes and lips that can be mixed and matched to yield more than 70,000 looks.

From customizable faces to athletic bods, *mannequins* bear a new likeness to the living.

Words **Jane Szita**

Even in this age of online retail, 42 per cent of shoppers admit (in a recent survey by NPD Group) that what they buy is influenced by in-store mannequin displays. No wonder then that brands are so eager to capitalize on the ability of these 'silent salespeople' to reflect their identity. 'The watchwords today are customization and uniqueness,' says Alfonso Catanese of Almax. 'The ability to customize a product plays a key role in relationships with luxury brands. We have a team of creatives and sculptors working with visual merchandisers from fashion brands, so we can meet any request.' Almax's latest catalogue of finishes showcases a wide range of dramatic handcrafted effects – including metal, resin, fabric, marble and wood – which can add an idiosyncratic edge to any retail environment.

Bonami's Danny Bonami agrees that modern mannequins, produced through a combination of traditional crafts and cutting-edge technologies, continue to play a vital role in the industry. 'The future of physical display products is still very much alive,' he says. 'Some clients order online after being impressed by an attractive window display.' Bonami's versatile and graceful Fashion Queens series, which can be completed with various styles of heads and even high-impact detachable Design Shoes, contributes to the kind of striking 3D display able to help retailers drive sales – not only in brick-and-mortar stores, but also online.

Andreas Gesswein, CEO of Genesis Mannequins, says that web shops impact mannequins by creating the need for 'more emotions and greater differentiation and fashion affinity' in physical stores. The company's extensive new ranges, Icon and New Generation, are available in a variety of colours and finishes, providing retailers with a wealth of options to tailor to their brand message. 'For the successful business, the future will certainly be a mix of online and stationary trade, and retail has to pay more attention than ever to image-building, emotions and brand positioning,' says Gesswein. 'Mannequins must adapt to this trend and implement the corresponding messages.'

'Due to the online offer, you need a reason to go out and buy a product in a retail space,' says Marco Ouwerkerk of Hans Boodt Mannequins (see page 218). 'The physical retail environment should offer an ever-changing and challenging experience.' Mannequins can play an important role in this, he adds, with a strong trend towards customization and emphasis on brand value. The company's latest collections – Celebrate Life and »

Complementing the natural and relaxed attitudes that characterize Theory – a collection of male and female mannequins from Proportion London – are soft features and slender forms.

Modelling realistic proportions and natural poses, the Noble line from Bonaveri – a collection of timeless male mannequins – avoids a look of exaggeration.

Blend Facet – therefore 'reflect a demand for high-end, specially designed products and the quest for individualization in current and bespoke products'.

Bust a Move

With athleisure continuing to play a prominent role in fashion, today's mannequin collections also demonstrate an increased sense of movement. 'Our new collection, LDN Girls, is a departure from the straight poses that have been so popular over the past few years,' says Caroline Kelly of Panache Display. The London company's creative team relied on street observation for the dynamism that marks LDN Girls: 'Walking around London, we were inspired by groups of girls, their animation and body language.' The fluid natural movement of the collection can be adapted to suit a wide variety of brand images, thanks to three head options and a variety of finishes.

'The industry is going through a period of change,' notes Alejandra Silva of Barcelona-based Atrezzo (see page 215). 'After years of minimalism and abstraction, we are heading towards a transition in materials, differentiation, colours and movement.' Physical energy is the theme of Atrezzo's Gym collection, which freeze-frames a series of running, skipping and stretching poses. The company's MKNO collection, meanwhile, opts for maximum movability, with highly articulated mannequins that are capable of extremely naturalistic movement. 'They can imitate any gesture, however extreme or subtle,' says Silva.

In Paris, Cofrad Mannequins is producing collections with the same dynamic tendency. 'Sport in fashion is a major trend today,' says Cofrad's Stéphanie Lacroix. 'It's part of everyday life. Our mannequins have chiselled and sculpted bodies coupled with dynamic and active poses.' Cofrad's Sport mannequins strike the action stances of runners, footballers, trekkers, boxers, body pumpers and a whole series of yogis, performing various asanas from the lotus to a gravity-defying scorpion. They are available in a series of chic matte finishes, including gold and slate. »

The future of physical display products is still very much alive

Danny Bonami, BONAMI

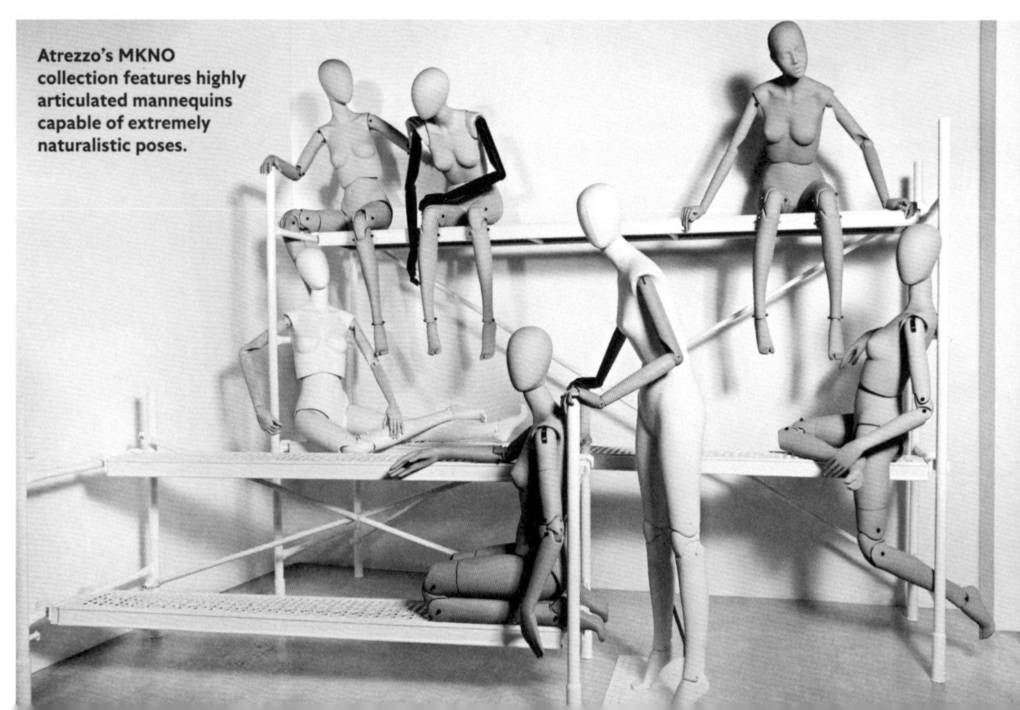

Atrezzo's MKNO collection features highly articulated mannequins capable of extremely naturalistic poses.

VENTURA
LAMBRATE
12–17 APRIL
WWW.VENTURAPROJECTS.COM
MILAN 2016

Bonami's versatile and customizable Fashion Queens series includes various styles of heads and accessories.

The athletic, sculpted bodies in Cofrad Mannequins' Sport series strike multiple action stances.

ABC Mannequins uses a direct-casting technique to create naturalistic forms and realistic attitudes.

At Rootstein, the new Défilé collection is based not on sport, but on a performance of a different kind: the fluid movements of models on the catwalk. 'What is lost in many display products is a sense of individuality, romance and a touch of coolness or drama,' says the company's Joe Tate. He points out that today's retailers have rather contradictory requirements in terms of mannequins: they want displays that are as high impact *and* as functional as possible: 'With our Défilé collection, we can meet both needs – the drama of realistic mannequins and the usability of abstract ones.'

Body Doubles

After a long period of domination by abstract mannequins, realism has returned with a vengeance – albeit in a softened, idealized form. Many manufacturers are showcasing modern wig and make-up options, as well as lifelike 'socializing' poses. ABC Mannequins uses the direct-casting technique – plaster is applied directly to the body of a live model – to create naturalistic forms and multiple realistic attitudes. Its Ophelia collection includes a female line available in 28 poses, plus a male series with a rapidly growing range of gestures. So much variety means that the collection can be used to assemble lifelike scenarios in which mannequins interact with one another. Customizable finishes enhance Ophelia's versatility. »

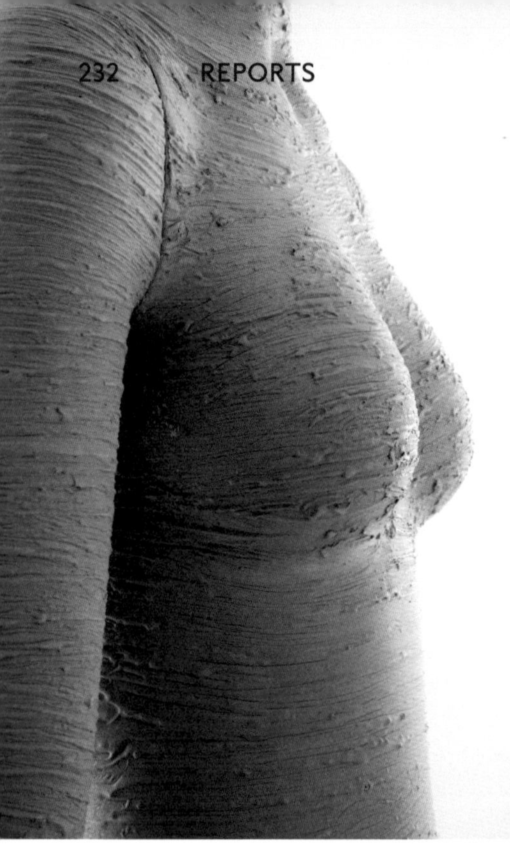

Almax's latest catalogue of finishes showcases a variety of dramatic handcrafted effects in metal, resin, fabric, marble and wood – a range with something to suit virtually any brand identity.

Distinctly androgynous, La Rosa's slender Q series challenges gender stereotypes.

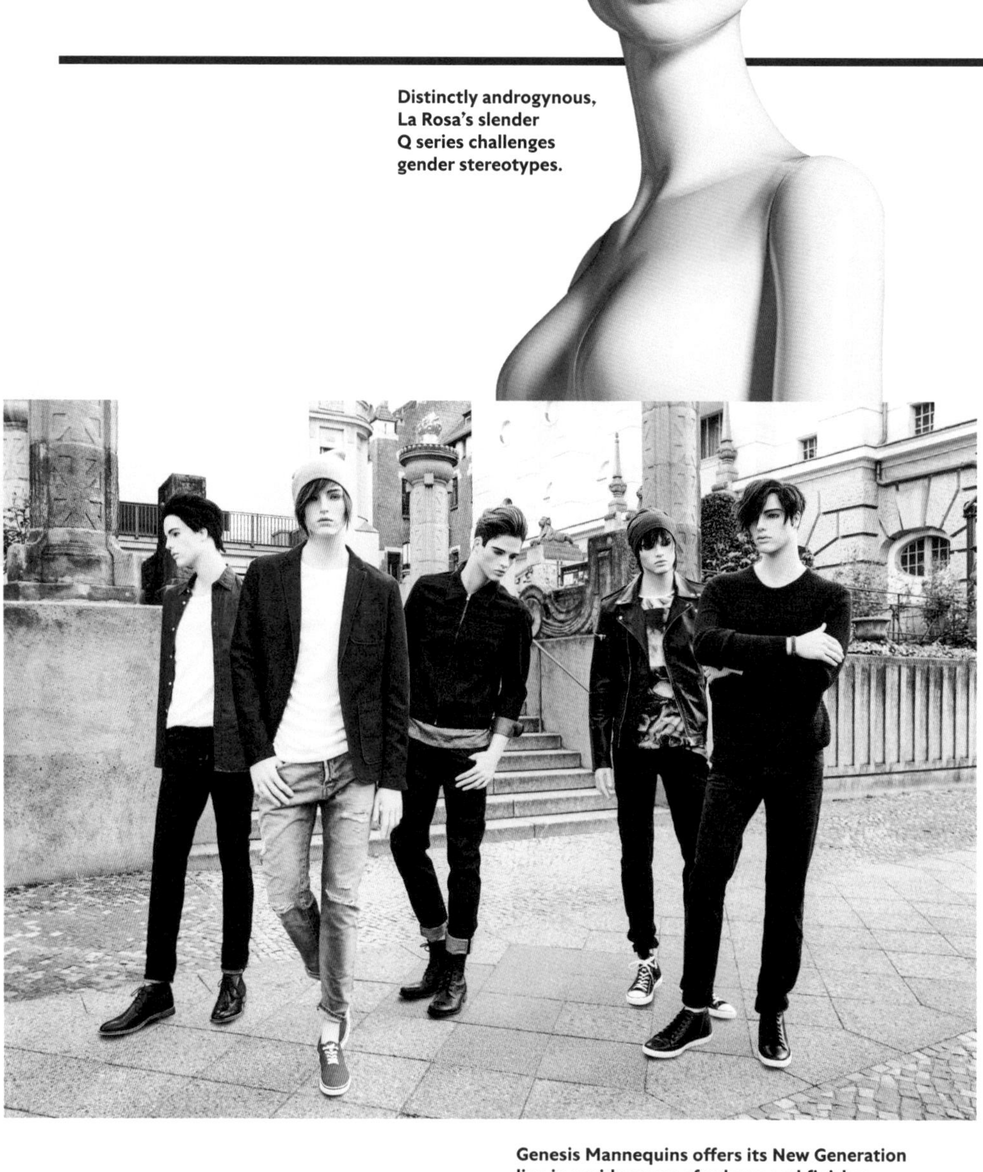

Genesis Mannequins offers its New Generation line in a wide range of colours and finishes, providing retailers with a wealth of options to tailor to their brand message.

Combining realism with abstraction generates fresh possibilities

Over at Bonaveri, Noble – a new male line for the Schläppi collection – pursues a similar idealized realism. Noble is intended to be the male companion to Aloof, Bonaveri's previously released Schläppi female series. 'We set out four guidelines for the development of Noble: a sense of presence, dedicated thought, elegance and an ability to group with other mannequins,' says Andrea Bonaveri. Noble avoids extremes to produce a timeless attitude, he adds, while the series is designed to work as a group, as well as individually, 'giving visual merchandisers and designers the opportunity to achieve unlimited combinations by arranging the mannequins in different groupings'.

Combining realism with abstraction generates fresh possibilities. Window Mannequin's Cameleon offers 'removable faces, eyes and lips to enable stores to create more than 70,000 styles from the same mannequin', says CEO Jean Marc Mesguich. Meanwhile, Window's Voluptuous 91 series reflects the fashion industry's ongoing challenge involving body stereotypes: the new line presents a more realistically sized, yet still glamorous, body type. The collection was designed in collaboration with a top plus-size model.

Gender stereotypes are also questioned in the new realism. La Rosa's lean Q collection is notably androgynous, and the company's Sabrina Ciofi calls it 'a milestone towards the definition of a new body type, typical of today's generation, which tends not to tolerate constraints in terms of name, category, age or gender'. The result is 'perfect for today's fashion standards' while remaining 'a neutral shell that speaks all the languages of the world and will prove commercially adaptable, yet also close to the fashion world'.

'The visual-merchandizing industry is at the forefront of the blurring of genders through provocative fashion presentation.' Speaking is Tanya Reynolds of Proportion London, whose male and female Theory collection obscures 'the lines between boy/girl fashion presentation'. The trend, she explains, is partly down to 'a more relaxed and educated set of consumers', but also to budget constraints: 'The display industry is a lot more savvy when it comes to buying and building chameleon presentation kits that can be reworked season after season.' Could morphing mannequins be the next big thing? ●

The EU *in*

Febrik teams up with *Edward van Vliet* in a dramatic demonstration of Dutch craftsmanship and pride.

Words **Will Georgi**

When Edward van Vliet was asked to design the venues for the Netherlands Presidency of the Council of the European Union, he turned to Febrik.

Blue

In addition to an expanded Sushi Collection in blue, red, green, and black and white, Febrik is launching Edward van Vliet's designs at the Salone del Mobile.

Textile company Febrik and Dutch designer Edward van Vliet go way back, all the way back to the brand's beginnings. The iconic Sushi Collection that Van Vliet designed for Moroso in 2008 was one of the first projects that put Febrik on the map as manufacturers of eye-catching knitted fabrics. As owner Jos Pelders proudly states: 'The Sushi Collection was really the icing on the cake.'

Both parties have come a long way since those heady days, but when Van Vliet – the 'pattern boy', as Pelders fondly calls him – was asked to do the interiors of three Amsterdam buildings earmarked as venues for delegates to the Netherlands Presidency of the Council of the European Union (which comes to a close in June), he turned to Febrik once more. Why? For the very same reasons he called upon the brand in 2008. He mentions not only 'the flexibility and versatility of Febrik's product', but also 'the stretchiness of the fabric, which makes it ideal for round shapes', while emphasizing that 'Febrik offers the possibility to develop both customized and standard collections'.

In his own words, Van Vliet 'designs total experiences' with a rich visual signature that is lavishly encapsulated in his book, *Creating Worlds*. Febrik's flexibility allows Van Vliet's imagination to run riot throughout the vast space of the EU Council's temporary home, where everything you see, from the carpets to a table that seats 84 ministers, is attributable to the Dutch designer.

'Edward loves making geometric patterns,' says Pelders. 'He plays with materials in such a natural and fun way. Take the Dutch Sky carpet, for example. He creates a special environment with everything he touches.' In this case, the result is an array of predominately blue (chosen to symbolize the host's maritime heritage) carpets and chairs upholstered in a series of customized, specially commissioned Febrik fabrics that illustrate his preference for expressive motifs.

'To help Edward lend shape to the worlds he envisioned, we played around with our techniques, eventually translating his ideas into tactile, usable textiles,' Pelders tells me. 'In this era, when everyone is looking for a way to stand out, the ability to develop unique materials is a real advantage. A surface material is the most immediate and emotional layer of an object. It's so in your face, especially the way Edward does it with his patterns.'

We're in his studio when Van Vliet shows me two unique Febrik fabrics of his own design. It's hard to resist caressing them as I admire the fine craftsmanship. They're just, well, different. Sadly, that's as close as most local citizens will get to the materials, as EU meeting rooms are closed to the public for security reasons. That's why Van Vliet is presenting his designs for Febrik at the Salone del Mobile: to share them with the rest of the world.

Febrik and Van Vliet are launching the new fabrics – as well as an expanded Sushi Collection in blue (as seen in Amsterdam), red, green, and black and white – at the Dutch Pavilion in Milan's Palazzo Turati. Pelders is thrilled. 'It's a nice way for Holland to show what it's capable of in terms of textiles, design and interior architecture,' he says. 'Just like everything Edward does, it stands out.' ●

creatingworlds.edwardvanvliet.com
febrik.com

From **Cloak** to **Shelter**

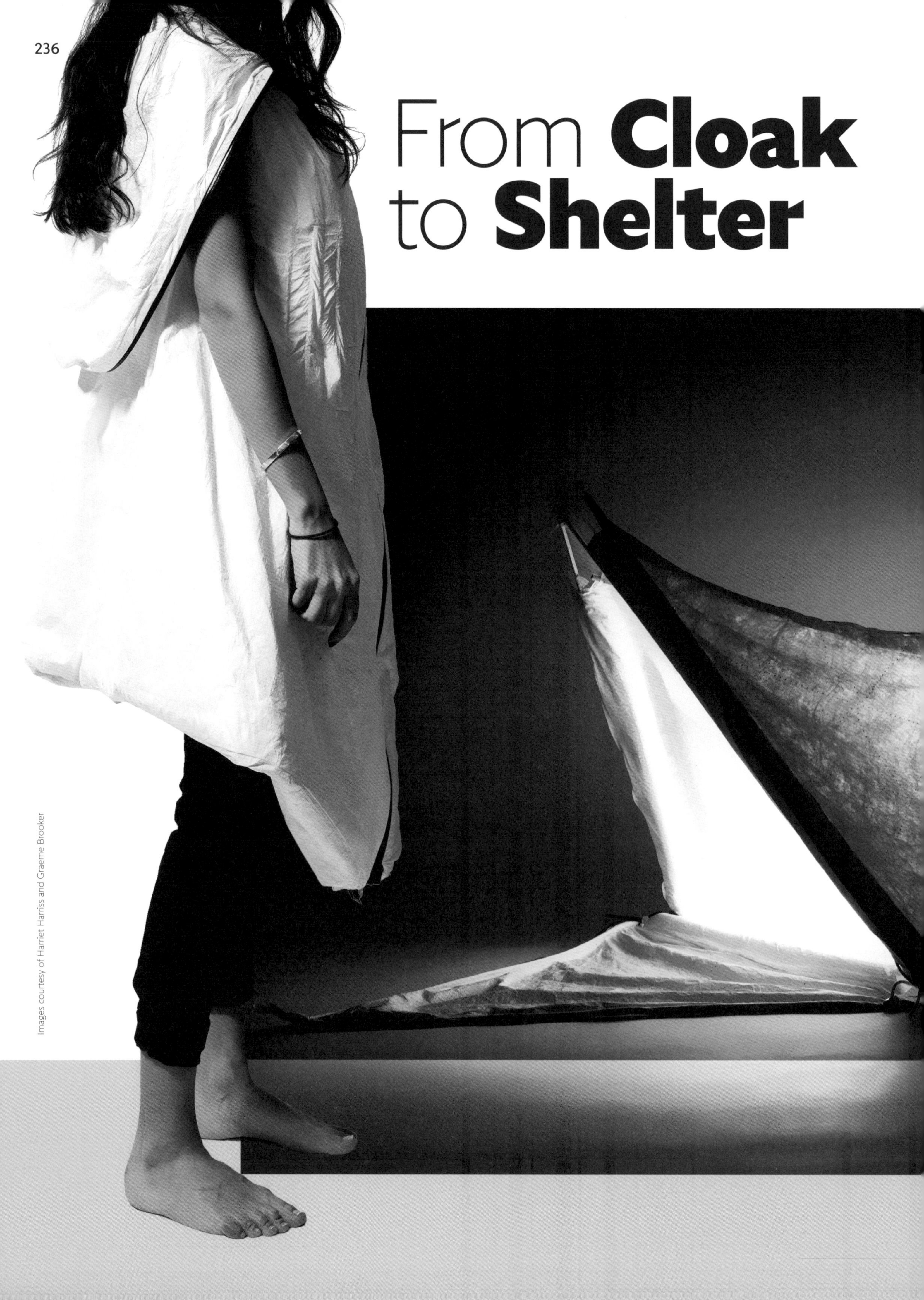

Images courtesy of Harriet Harriss and Graeme Brooker

RCA students reveal their first prototype of a *wearable dwelling for refugees.*

Words **Will Georgi**

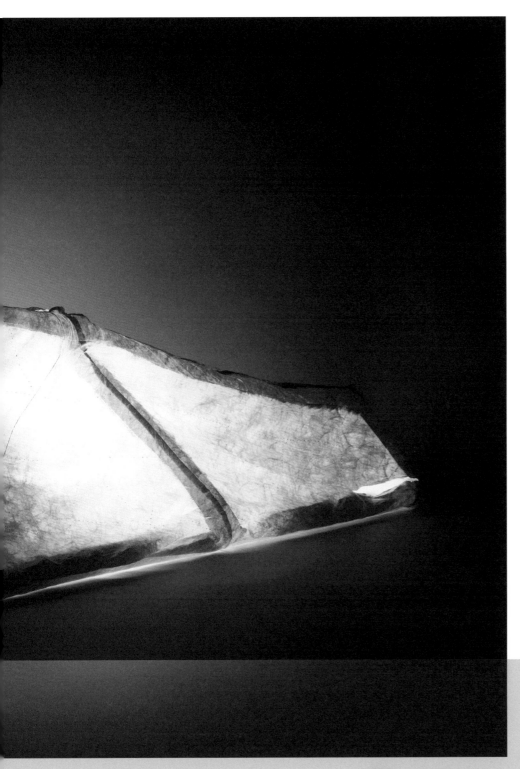

As demonstrated by the sea of lifejackets littering the Mediterranean coastlines, the Syrian refugee crisis isn't going away anytime soon. The question of how to provide the displaced with adequate food and shelter has rocked Europe to its core. Can designers help? 'Yes,' say Harriet Harriss and Graeme Brooker, lecturers at London's Royal College of Art. 'Good design isn't just about technologies and devices. It has a social heart and a role to play in meeting the needs of people facing impossible challenges.'

Fuelled by the current emergency, Harriss and Brooker tasked interior-design and textile students at the RCA with the creation of a 'wearable habitation' for refugees. The students based their project on migrants' circumstances and needs. A hybrid union of jacket, sleeping bag and tent, the final prototype was developed in collaboration with humanitarian organization Médecins Sans Frontières (Doctors Without Borders), which gave the designers an insight into the practical problems faced by desperate people fleeing warzones. Issues of mobility and weathering meant that materials had to be both tough and lightweight. The inner lining of the 'coat' is a polyester film normally used for insulation, and the outer surface is made from Tyvek, a synthetic nonwoven commonly used for damp-proofing buildings during construction.

The team hopes its multifunctional result will not only help refugees on the ground but also raise awareness of the importance of finding an integrated long-term solution for the growing crisis. Despite financial help received from Wall Fashion London, the garment-cum-shelter cannot go into full production without further funding. ●

rca.ac.uk

FRAME

Go to the digital magazine to watch a tent transform into a coat

National **Treasure**

The official seat for the 1939 Swiss National Exhibition, Hans Coray's *Landi Chair returns to its roots* **with Vitra.**

Words **Enya Moore** Illustration **Sam Green**

Hans Coray

Born in Wald, Switzerland, Hans Coray was brought up in Zurich, where he studied Romance languages. He worked as a secondary-school teacher before entering the design world upon winning a competition for seating to be used at the 1939 Swiss National Exhibition. In his later years, he turned his attention to painting and sculpture.

At the end of the 1939 Swiss National Exhibition, visitors could buy a Landi Chair for a 5 franc coin.

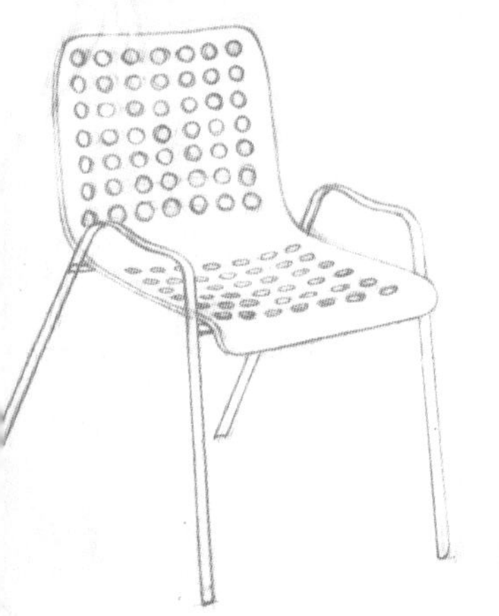

No fewer than 91 holes puncture the shell of the Landi Chair, circular openings that give the seat its characteristic appearance and make it lightweight.

“The Landi Chair has a sketch-like quality and a likable personality

Eckart Maise

After almost 80 years the Landi Chair, designed by Swiss artist and designer Hans Coray, has finally found a place to call home. Originally designed as the official chair of the 1939 Swiss National Exhibition, the seat was pioneering in its use of aluminium, a material whose possibilities for the furniture industry were only then becoming apparent. Made and marketed intermittently by various companies since its inception, the Landi is now back in production under the experienced eye of Swiss furniture giant Vitra.

According to Eckart Maise, chief design officer at Vitra, the manufacture of this chair was a long-held desire of the company. Rolf Fehlbaum, chairman of Vitra, had discussed the prospect with Coray in the 1980s, but before the opportunity eventually arose a few years ago, Coray had died. In a bid to realize a product that was in line with Coray's original vision, the team at Vitra worked closely with his wife, Henriette.

'The chair has quite a long and fragmented production history, so together with Henriette Coray we examined all iterations of the chair from different eras, in order to arrive at the purest expression of the design,' says Maise. In addition to her personal recollections, Henriette was able to provide drawings, sketches and even a long letter that Coray had written about the chair. Vitra not only honed the design but also streamlined the production process. For example, the thick edge of the shell is now made robotically instead of manually, a change that raises the level of precision.

'Even though the Landi Chair was created using a cold, industrial material, it has a sketch-like quality and a very likable personality,' says Maise. Perhaps it is the chair's pleasant character, instilled by Coray, that is Landi's most enduring legacy. ●

vitra.com

Paper **Chain**

Studio Front's cut-out collection for Eco Wallpaper *drapes, weaves and layers* **through today's interiors.**

Words **Christian Walters**

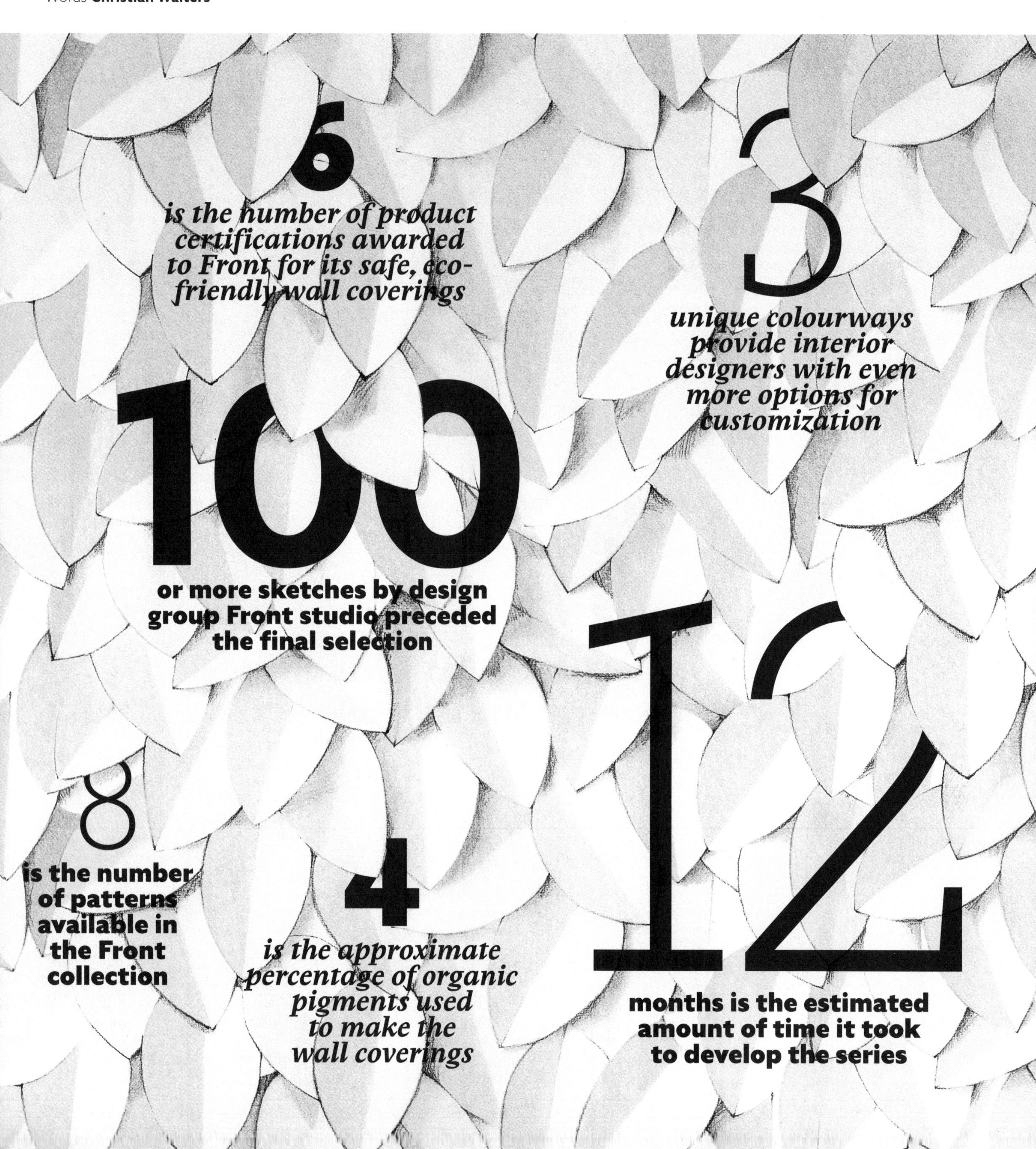
6
is the number of product certifications awarded to Front for its safe, eco-friendly wall coverings
3
unique colourways provide interior designers with even more options for customization
100
or more sketches by design group Front studio preceded the final selection
12
months is the estimated amount of time it took to develop the series
8
is the number of patterns available in the Front collection
4
is the approximate percentage of organic pigments used to make the wall coverings